The
Suicidal
Patient

The Suicidal Patient:

Recognition and
Management

Ari Kiev, M.D.

Nelson-Hall
Chicago

Library of Congress Cataloging in Publication Data

Kiev, Ari.
    The suicidal patient

    Bibliography: p.
    Includes index.
    1.   Suicide—United States.   2. Suicide—United
States—Prevention.   I. Title. [DNLM: 1. Suicide.
2. Suicide, Attempted.   HV6545.K47L]
HV6548.U5K54   364.4   76–47330
ISBN 0–88229–302–8

Copyright © 1977 by Ari Kiev

All rights reserved. No part of this book may be reproduced
in any form without permission in writing from the publisher,
except by a reviewer who wishes to quote brief passages in
connection with a review written for broadcast or for inclusion
in a magazine or newspaper. For information address Nelson-Hall
Inc., Publishers; 325 West Jackson Boulevard; Chicago, Illinois
60606.

Manufactured in the United States of America.

Only rarely is human behavior governed by one tendency only. The outcome of most human actions, especially of most irrational [ones] such as suicidal acts, depends on the quantitative relationship of conflicting tendencies and on many other actions, some of them unpredictable. Only in a small minority of people who commit suicidal acts is the self-destructive urge so overwhelming that it completely submerges those tendencies which aim at human contact and preservation of life.

Erwin Stengel

Contents

Preface

THE number of suicide attempts in the United States is estimated to be about 200,000. The number of people who have attempted suicide during their lifetime is estimated to be about 2,000,000 (Dublin, 1963; Stengel and Cook, 1958; Stengel, 1962; Tabachnick and Farberow, 1961; Rubenstein, Moses, and Lidz, 1958). The high incidence of suicidal behavior constitutes a major public health problem, recognition of which is attested to by the development of suicide prevention programs at federal, state, and local levels. The present work is the result of an investigation designed to identify the crucial variables in the natural history of attempted suicides that might prove relevant to preventive programs and objectives.

The most striking result of our investigation has been the observation that suicidal behavior is generally not understood by the vast majority of people.

This book seeks to clarify the major dimensions of the

phenomenon of attempted suicide by illuminating the avenues for prevention. It is possible to recognize each step in the natural history of attempted suicide and expeditiously handle the patient's problems so as to avoid the suicidal crisis. Prevention may be introduced when the first signs of depression appear; when the patient begins to pursue a self-destructive course of self-medication, excessive alcohol, or drug abuse. It may be introduced at the time interpersonal conflict evolves; still later, after a suicide attempt has occurred, preventive efforts may be introduced to modify the persisting interpersonal conflict. Finally, after a suicide attempt, the treatment and follow-up become critical in preventing repeated episodes.

A suicide attempt frequently occurs when the usual methods of coping with life's problems have failed and/or when maladaptive efforts complicate an individual's experience and impair even the ability to utilize habitual coping methods. While such a situation can often prove disastrous, it can also be a turning point. A suicide attempt can serve to alert the person to important and soluble problems that had previously been obscure. It can be a turning point, especially if the individual seeks professional help. Often such a suicidal crisis may lead to the discovery that a person has been suffering from an untreated chronic depression that simply had not been recognized.

A suicidal crisis can provide a stimulus for the individual to take a new and different look at himself and his relationships with others. Frequently, more healthy and satisfying ways of living and relating to others can evolve from the changes that take place during and after a suicide attempt. But for changes to occur, there must be an understanding of the total complex of operative factors and the ways in which they impinge on the individual.

There is considerable need for both medical personnel and lay people to be more informed about the phenomenon of suicide. The subject must be examined in broad daylight, especially if we are to help those who know of someone who might be suicidal.

It is hoped that this book, which examines the variety of events leading to suicide, may serve to demythologize the subject. It examines the social, psychological, historical, and phenomenological characteristics of suicidal behavior; how patients should be treated; what must be done to alleviate symptoms to reduce pressure; how to recognize a potential suicidal person and what to do about it; what kinds of programs can be set up around the country.

Chapter I

Theoretical Background— Historical Viewpoints

WHY do people attempt suicide? Numerous sociological, psychological, theological, and philosophical theories of suicide have been proposed to explain suicidal behavior. Almost all of these theories have assumed that suicide had a meaning and could be explained in terms of such things as the religious or social order or in terms of individual psychopathology. Few of these theories have been based on a careful analysis of the empirical evidence. Most have derived from general theories of human behavior or from philosophical views on such questions as free will and individual responsibility. Albert Camus, the famous existentialist writer and philosopher, viewed the question of suicide as the "one truly serious philosophical question."

In the eighteenth century, writers including Montaigne, Donne, and Hume, who emphasized individual over societal responsibility, argued that each individual had a right to take his or her own life. This view contrasted with the longstanding religious notion that the individual had absolutely no right to take his own life and that suicide was a serious sin against God, if not a crime against the state. A shift in attitude toward suicide occurred in the nineteenth century when suicide was included in the vital statistics of society and as such just began to be considered a manifestation of social pathology.

The nineteenth-century penchant for social statistics led many to observe regularities in the rates of suicide which, in turn, supported the notion that some unknown social factors (over and above free will) accounted for suicide. Scholars began to theorize that social factors influenced individual action and that general laws could be developed to explain human behavior much as the law of nature explained the physical world.

The nineteenth-century tradition of keeping statistics of such events as suicide thus fostered a search for social explanations of the regularity of suicide rates. The implication of observable and undesirable social factors such as poverty, migration, unemployment, and anomie as causes of suicide, dominated the writings of the most prominent nineteenth-century French sociologist, Émile Durkheim.

Like other nineteenth-century writers, Durkheim attributed the rising suicide rate to a decline in the moral control society exercised on individuals. Integrating various social explanations, Durkheim theorized that suicide varied inversely with the degree of integration of the individual's group membership. High rates of social disorganization thus correlated with high rates of suicide.

Durkheim focused on the relationship between suicide rates and the amount of social disorganization in society as a major theoretical model for understanding suicide rates. Social disorganization is extremely difficult to measure independently, yet most investigators have been influenced enough by Durkheim to examine the relationship between high suicide rates and other indices of social disorganization.

Since Durkheim, other sociological studies have related high suicide rates to a decline in church membership, social mobility, social anonymity, reduced rates of social contacts (Cavan, 1949) as well as increased rates of divorce and illegitimacy (Sainsbury, 1956).

Quite clearly, social processes contribute in various ways to self-destructive behavior. Thus, to the extent that social disorganization correlates with a higher suicide rate, one can expect to find a higher incidence of disruptive social relations (or other features of social disorganization) in individual cases than in individuals who do not attempt suicide.*

Psychological explanations of suicide reached their most detailed form in various psychodynamic formulations developed in the twentieth century.

In this century, the numerous psychological explanations of self-destructive behavior developed by psychiatrists included such hypotheses as the following: excessive guilt from a punitive conscience (Hendin, 1954); hostility turned inward (Menninger, 1938); hope of rebirth or reunion with the dead to eliminate certain disturbing feelings of anger, grief, revenge, fear, envy, and the like, and/or to bring about certain effects, for example, to punish mothers by inducing their guilt, in order to escape from real or anticipated pain, loss of esteem, emotional distress, and/or for a number of additional, more complex, psychological reasons.

These formulations have largely been influenced by the psychoanalytic theory, first postulated by Freud, that suicide resulted from a depressive reaction precipitated by the loss of a significant relationship due to death, rejection,

---

*It should be noted that noxious environments may produce a range of disorders; specific disorders may arise from various social problems and social contexts.

disappointment, or even symbolic fantasy. This loss—activating an infantile drive to symbolically recapture (through psychological mechanisms of identification and introjection) the lost love object—provided the motive behind the suicide act.

Failure to transfer feelings to another love object and the propensity to use these "defense mechanisms" occur most frequently in certain types of people who customarily respond to loss with feelings of rejection and with anger directed inward, as well as to the symbolically internalized object.

Such people characteristically depend too much on others for affection, respect, and gratification and often harbor unexpressed resentment toward them and experience a real or fantasized loss of this support. The image of the important person or persons casts a shadow (identification) on the subject's ego. Finally, aggression toward the object is then directed toward the subject's own ego; a so-called splitting of the ego results.

Expanding on Freud's view, Menninger (1938) postulated multiple motives for suicide: a wish to kill the internalized object, but also a wish to be killed and a punitive conscience that causes feelings of guilt, self-hatred, self-punishment, and a wish to die.

Other psychoanalytic writers—Horney (1945), Sullivan (1953), and Adler (1964)—viewed suicide as an effort to validate a lifestyle, and as a refusal to accept the status quo. The suicidal person, when threatened, destroys himself physically to preserve his psychological reality.

In effect, the inability to meet environmental expectations creates feelings of helplessness and hopelessness and suicide becomes the only feasible way to resolve the conflict. Surviving the attempt, which symbolically destroys what exists, leads to a rebirth of hope, according to Wall (1944).

Social psychiatric approaches to the problem of self-destruction seek to integrate both the sociological and the psychological theories in an effort to develop rational preventive strategies that encompass all factors included in the patient's distress. In the past decade, this orientation has led to a focus on interpersonal factors impinging on the individual prior to, and at the time of, the suicidal crisis. Social psychiatric studies examine the factors in the individual's adaptation that may have created the crisis, e.g., ways, in which as a result of personality characteristics or a psychiatric illness, the suicidal person may have induced others in his or her social world to respond in negative ways which, in turn, may have been experienced as a rejection or loss of a "love object." Such styles of influencing others are learned early in life, and reinforced in later life by repetition of identical patterns of interaction. At times, the responses of others generate unsatisfactory feelings and experiences in the patient who cannot escape the relationship. This leads to an increase of inner tension and anxiety and sometimes collapse. In effect, social psychiatry focuses on a process of interaction between patient and environment searching for suitable points where therapeutic leverage may be exerted.

Certain phenomena at the onset of psychiatric illness trigger environmental responses that influence individual behavior. In this way, the evaluative and normative responses of the environment condition suicidal behavior. These same evaluative and normative standards apply under ordinary circumstances giving each individual some sense of the validity and legitimacy of his or her existence. Accepting this, we can begin to see what kind of impact the breakdown of the family can have on a young ghetto-dweller or how the inculcation of competitive achievement values may create conflict for ghetto-dwellers in their youth. We can also begin to see how social and cultural values give meaning even to the self-destructive alcoholism and the sometimes violent behavior of reservation Indians.

We know that elderly people living isolated lives in anomic transitional zones kill themselves with great frequency. Quite likely loss of community supports can be critical for those who are ill-prepared to cope on their own and for whom isolation has additional social meaning of rejection.

Chapter II

Psychological Problems

SUICIDE attempts rarely occur without some background of depressive symptoms. Feelings of helplessness, self-depreciation, emptiness, isolation, persecution, interpersonal conflict, rejection, and frustration tend to predominate among the subjective experiences of people who attempt suicide.

Occasionally, the attempt occurs as symptoms lift, a return of energy-facilitating action. This may at times be related to the fact that the decision to commit suicide resolves uncertainty and withdrawal and reduces depressive symptoms. Suicidal behavior may be associated with agitation, restlessness, and anxiety as well as with overactivity and lack of inhibitions. One cannot easily specify the exact time of onset of suicidal drive in relationship to the onset of depression since rarely does a depressive illness follow a uniform course or duration. Fluctuations in mood and energy commonly occur while the duration of episodes varies. Suicidal behavior also occurs in association with suicidal fantasies, catastrophic and self-destructive dreams, delusional expressions of guilt, marked hypochondriasis, and sudden life crises, all of which may trigger a sense of personal hopelessness and the meaninglessness of life.

In some people suicidal attempts occur most often in conjunction with early personality change and ego disintegration. The patient, terrified by the clash of the real world and his inner world, can no longer rationalize distorted perceptions. Sudden shifts in the patient's environment often produce hallucinations and paranoid delusions that increase suicidal risk.

Distorted perceptions may be prominent in certain people. Sonia D. attempted suicide by jumping into the East River with her baby. For months she had seen eyes looking at her, telling her to die. Depression, sleep loss, and inability to function resulted. She denied any intent to die, instead attributing her action to supernatural causes that she was compelled to obey. She saved herself because she could not kill her baby and swam to shore holding up her child.

People with lifelong problems in adjustment are often deficient in their capacity to trust others or to relate to them. Inability to establish meaningful relationships may lead to self-destructive trends during periods of stress. Their lifestyles may become the focus of pathological processes as a result of their inability to learn from experience. Rarely do they manifest discrete episodes of symptoms. Rather, repeated difficulties foster mild depressive symptoms in the form of discouragement, a negative self-image, passivity, dependency, and self-destructive behavior.

A typical history reveals a noxious family background and problematic interpersonal relationships. One or both parents may have alcoholic problems; they are cold, rejecting, and critical of the patient, discouraging any efforts to obtain professional help,

Such patients may enter treatment reluctantly because of an unwillingness to trust and accept help and support from others. Such patients account for a large percentage of failed treatment experiences. Prior to a suicide attempt, these patients become progressively more withdrawn, helpless, and dependent on others.

Often negative or self-destructive fantasies are reinforced and the suicide drive intensified by friends and relatives who cannot tolerate the increasing emotionality and helplessness of the patient. Failure to recognize the patient's distress may produce undesirable effects. The patient often assumes a martyr role that encourages others to impose even more burdens on him. In turn, the patient's hostile and self-destructive fantasies become more intense.

Factors contributing to suicidal behavior in the elderly, who have the highest suicide rates of any age group, include: depression, cerebral changes, confusion, poor judgment, low tension tolerance, difficult life situations, physical change, increasing isolation, a feeling of a vanishing and meaningless life, the resurgence of neurotic behavioral patterns, a diminution of aggressive outlets, and an inclination to attribute depressive symptoms to old age or illness, and, as such, to neglect treatment.

Our own investigation included the intensive evaluation and follow-up of 300 self-selected patients admitted to the inpatient or outpatient service of the Payne Whitney Clinic of the New York Hospital Cornell Medical Center or referred directly to our research unit. The patients were predominantly young men and women, with clinically manifest depressive symptomatology, who were involved in a series of life crises associated with faulty or unsatisfactory relationships. The majority, diagnosed as psychoneurotic depressive reactions or as character disorders, were functioning at work, in school, or in the home. Two percent were considered too disabled to function, and only twelve percent were temporarily unemployed.

Patients could be conveniently divided into three different groups which differed in a number of significant ways.

PSYCHOTIC GROUP

One group (19 percent of total cohort) consisted of patients with lifelong histories of severe psychopathology, multiple life stresses, family problems, and social isolation. In our studies, this group had significantly higher scores on a number of symptoms than did the other two patient groups. They had higher scores on anxiety, emotional withdrawal, conceptual disorganization, hostility, suspiciousness, hallucinatory behavior, unusual thought content, blunted affect, excitement, disorientation, sexual functioning, and obsessional thoughts.

This psychotic group had considerably higher ratings on lethality, isolation, overall and functioning. From a clinical viewpoint, the suicidal drive in this group appeared to evolve over time as individual vulnerability to stress progressively increased and coping ability decreased.

These patients experienced stress throughout the entire range of stress scores. A larger percentage of psychotic patients had minimal objective stresses in the year prior to their suicide attempt than did patients with depressive reactions or character disorders.

CHARACTER DISORDER

The second group of patients (33.67 percent of total cohort), variously described as "impulsive," "immature," "hysterical," or "inadequate," often gave a history of multiple attempts associated with minor objective stresses. These patients scored higher on ratings of alcohol abuse and drug abuse than the other two groups. A slightly greater percentage of these patients attempted suicide in close proximity to sources of help, and a larger percentage of these patients made efforts to reverse the situation after the attempt.

Unlike the stress scores of the psychotic group which were evenly distributed over the mild to severe range, the stress scores of character disorder and depressed patients peaked at the mild to moderate range of stress scores; 33.3 percent of character disorders as compared to 23.8 percent of depressed patients reported minimal objective stress in the preceding year. Unlike depressed patients, none of the character disorder patients reported severe stress.

DEPRESSIVE REACTION

The third group (44.67 percent of the total cohort) consisted of patients with unremarkable histories who attempted suicide in the setting of a depressive illness associated with major objective life stresses. A larger percentage of these patients were forty-six and older; 57.4 percent described severe objective stress as compared to 34.4 percent of character disorders and 42.3 percent of psychotics. The most commonly reported stresses were:

1. Serious emotional upset (breakup with boy/girl friend).
2. Failure to live up to the expectations of others.
3. Change in life settings.
4. Loss of loved one by death.
5. Loss of loved one by divorce or separation.
6. Marital conflict.

The above findings suggested that diagnostic factors functioned as mediating variables between precipitating stresses and suicidal behavior. The finding that a greater percentage of depressed control patients experienced major objective stresses (e.g., death of a loved one, serious illness) than the other patient groups, a greater percentage of whom reported stresses that were not totally independent

of their own behavior, suggested further that early exposure to stress experiences may be as important in influencing suicidal behavior as the immediate precipitating stresses.

MOST COMMON SYMPTOMS ON INITIAL EVALUATION

The majority of patients reported a wide range of mild to severe symptoms of anxiety and depression. The most common symptom, depressed mood, occurred in moderate to severe form in 90.2 percent of all patients. The next most common symptom reported was anxiety; 82.3 percent reported moderate to severe anxiety. Similar distributions of scores were reported for other symptoms as well. The frequency distributions of symptoms are displayed in Table 2.

As expected, severe symptoms of grandiosity, suspiciousness, unusual thoughts, hallucinations, mannerisms, and conceptual disorganization occurred most often in the psychotic diagnostic group. Psychotic patients also complained more frequently of severe obsessive thoughts, suicidal thoughts, loss of sexual drive, appetite disturbances, sleep disturbances, guilt, tension, conceptual disorganization, anxiety, social withdrawal, and somatic symptoms than did the depressed patients or character disorder patients.

Depressed patients complained more frequently of severe depressive mood. Character disorder patients received more severe scores for social withdrawal, tension, and guilt than depressed patients.

MODERATE SYMPTOMS

Anxiety and depression led the list of symptoms which occurred most frequently with moderate severity. The frequency distribution of anxiety, tension, depressed mood, and suicidal thoughts was higher for persons with character disorders than for either the depressed or the psychotic patients.

OVERALL FUNCTIONING

The extent of impaired functioning was far greater than might have been anticipated on the basis of the patient's psychopathology; 27.3 percent of the patients were hospitalized; 11.3 percent reported that symptoms led to lack of performance; 19.3 percent reported symptoms limiting capacity to cope with most major responsibilities; 21.7 percent could not meet all responsibilities. The hospitalized group included 40.4 percent of the psychotic, 29.7 percent of character disorders, and 24 percent of depressed patients.

Chapter III

Methods

THE ambivalent nature of the suicide attempt is suggested by the fact that the majority of patients make an effort to reverse the situation by seeking or calling for help. There are various forms of suicide, the nature of the act depending on the psychological issues involved—when it occurs in the course of an individual's life experience, when it occurs in relationship to thoughts about it, and the like. Most people call someone immediately, race to a hospital, call a doctor, or call a suicide prevention center. A small percentage of people wait for someone to arrive expecting indeed that someone was on his or her way.

Most attempted suicides occur at home, a friend's home, or at work. Only a very few choose an impersonal location such as a park or a bridge. Indeed, the majority of attempts occur with someone close by or easily accessible. Only a small number attempt suicide when others are at a distance. Where individuals communicate intent to suicide, they are found to have passive-aggressive or passive-dependent personality traits rather than severe depression —which more often retards individual action. Such patients characteristically involve others in their actions and do so in relationship to the suicide act, less as a cry of help, more as a result of their characteristic dependency. Of interest, when the attempt occurs in a location that is removed from possible help, the prognosis for a repeated and more serious attempt is greater.

WHAT ARE THE MOST COMMON METHODS EMPLOYED IN SUICIDE ATTEMPTS?

Self-poisoning by an overdose of medication accounted for the majority of attempted suicides in our sample of 300. Lacerations accounted for 18 percent of cases, and this was followed by much smaller numbers who attempted suicide with gas, poison, jumping, or the use of a gun.

These figures correspond to the frequency distributions found in most suicide prevention clinics.

Method	Number	Percent
Pills	209	69.67
Lacerations	54	18.
Gas	8	2.76
Poison	10	3.33
Jump	17	5.67
Gun	2	.67

Self-poisoning with sedatives and tranquilizers is the most common method used in suicide attempts. Some individuals consciously ingest sufficient amounts to kill themselves. Others seek only to escape pressure, giving little thought to the possibility of death. They may swallow more and more pills solely to maximize the tranquilizing or sedative effects of the pills, without regard for the consequences. Alcohol, which reduces the inhibitions of self-destructive drives, may accentuate the negative effects of such extreme self-medication.

Unpredictability is a characteristic feature of suicide attempts. Panic, depersonalization, and mental disorganization often characterize the early stages of acute suicidal crises. An intense and unpleasant state of tension and anxiety and a temporary cessation of ego functions that cannot be consciously controlled occur in these earlier stages. Altered levels of consciousness may occur as well, making rational thought difficult if not impossible once the process is set in motion.

Describing this depersonalized state, one young woman said: "It's just emotions running in two completely diverse directions and there's no tie between myself and anything else. It's a loss of identity. Different things set it off and it's weird. It's sort of anxiety. It's like all the torture and shit that I've experienced. My mind goes completely blank. I am not there. I am not at home. I am literally not in contact with anything. You could probably come up to me at that point and say, 'Let's go to China,' and I would go. And I figured the depersonalization and torture have always been rejection, and it's been happening since I was a kid. I used to get locked in my room, but I used to sit there and sit there for hours and hours and that was my whole world. I never knew about reality."

Episodes of elation or excitement often blend indistinguishably with a chaotic life situation and are frequently associated with attempted suicide. Irritability and hyperactivity often precipitate interpersonal crises and arguments that lead to impulsive acts of aggression or self-destruction.

Some people experience acute and transient mood swings secondary to environmental pressures. Short-lived suicidal drives occur when they are in a depressed-mood state and disappear as rapidly, a fact, no doubt, accounting for the high discharge rate of suicide attempts from hospital emergency rooms, the minimization of the need for aftercare provision, and the frequency of repeated attempts under similar social circumstances. The brevity of the risk period makes it difficult to recognize the risk and to prevent the suicidal behavior.

Wrist slashing tends to become a repetitive act. Marked tension, unrelieved by medicine or activity, usually accompanies such attempts. Patients in such tension states ignore the self-inflicted pain during the episode, but later suffer considerable discomfort and pain as well as remorse, helplessness, and shame. Wrist slashing is a potentially lethal self-inflicted injury. Most wrist slashers deny conscious intent to kill themselves, emphasizing instead fear of not being able to control their behavior. This potential for uncontrolled behavior provokes significant others to limit the patient's freedom, which intensifies tension and perpetuates a vicious cycle. Inability to accept responsibility, fear of criticism, and resentment of the intrusions of others characterize the psychodynamic issues involved in the interpersonal relationships of such patients.

Repetitive attempts usually take the same form and are most commonly seen in young men and women motivated by a desire to reduce unbearable tension rather than to die. Hair pulling, skin biting, skin scratching, and other mutilations frequently precede repeated suicide attempts. The support of others can reduce the tension.

Angry or punitive responses increase the tension. The response patterns of others often become intricately interwoven with the self-destructive behavior and influence the repetitive nature of these attempts. According to the wife of one patient: "He plays for sympathy and when he doesn't get it, he gets mad. He's been feeling lousy. He's very negative. He couldn't sleep Wednesday night. He was jittery, and I haven't seen him this bad since before he went into the hospital.

"I think this is the longest he's been out of work. He

does nothing but dwell on himself all day. The restlessness irritates him and he feels uncomfortable. He doesn't know what to do with the feeling of discomfort. Then he starts complaining, which really upsets me more than his feeling of discomfort. His discomfort means that he wants sympathy from me. He becomes annoyed and uptight."

Repetitive attempts can be dangerous, particularly when an individual loses self-control while under the influence of alcohol or has evoked strong reactions from others. Some patients attempting to escape into sleep take more and more pills when lower doses are ineffective. Some panic when the sedative produces a loss of ego control but no sleep.

"It takes a lot of energy to fight your problems. I didn't feel as though I were capable of it. I was conscious of what I was doing. I didn't just recklessly grab the razor blade. First of all, I turned on the gas, put paper around the kitchen floor, closed the windows, and put a curtain up against the window. I felt very much at home until I realized that it wasn't working, that I had gone this far. I guess I was very dizzy as a result of the gas and still feeling very depressed. I grabbed the razor blade, feeling so dizzy that I didn't have time to think. I thought that if I didn't succeed that I would still be able to operate my hand. I was 100 percent set on killing myself. Right after that I became shocked by the realization that I had completed this act. I *panicked* and I called a friend. When I saw the blood, I panicked.

"At first, they didn't see the cut at all. Then they rushed me up to Manhattan State Hospital but they had no room. Upon seeing the cut wrist they immediately called two police officers and they tried questioning my friend and myself. Then we were taken down to Bellevue Hospital where the cut was examined by a physician. I am not sure whether he was a surgeon or not, a medical psychiatrist, or a doctor of medicine, but he looked at it. It was then dressed. I was taken up to Ward PQ, and up there I had to fend for myself. Within thirty-six hours I had been asked about what I had done six or seven times, very demandingly. Bellevue was such a frightful place, so unsanitary. I was afraid to sit on the toilet and wash my hands, even eat, you know, with people who had open sores. Then the next morning I woke up. I remember going to bed, my heart pounding like crazy and feeling very flushed and thinking this would take me out of my misery. I'm gone. I turned the light off, but then I woke up. The next day I said, 'Oh Lord, what are you keeping me alive for?' "

Shooting, drowning, hanging, and gas inhalation account for a large percentage of completed suicide attempts. Studying patients who survive attempts with these methods provides some perspective on the mental state of patients who die from such methods. The inference drawn is that patients who choose dangerous methods often do so without having the most serious intent. Violent attempts are generally highly impulsive, but there is no evidence that these patients are more intent on killing themselves than those who use less dangerous methods.

Some dangerous attempts appear to be sudden and impulsive but in fact are the culmination of weeks of withdrawal and rumination that totally absorb the patient and eventually govern his or her impulses. Active interpersonal conflict may precipitate a number of impulsive, dramatic, and desperate attempts. Some individuals lack the self-restraint to stop themselves once they have moved to the brink of a dangerous situation. One young man, P. K. K., made such a high-risk attempt. En route from a New Jersey hospital to a New York psychiatric hospital, he forced his way out of the car door as it crossed the George Washington Bridge, leaped several barriers, and jumped from the bridge into the freezing water. He was fortunately able to swim to the shore.

Careful examination revealed that he had grown suspicious of others and distrusted everyone who he believed were "part of a plot to get me." He had no fear that he would lose his life for as he said, "I knew the Good Lord would save me."

Other very dangerous attempts in our own studies have included a middle-aged businessman who was recovering from a depression and was seemingly well when he went to his basement and shot himself in his chest; R. S., a young pregnant woman with a past history of depression and suicidal behavior who shot herself in the head when her expressions of suicidal urges were ignored by her husband; B. G., a fifty-year-old woman who tried to electrocute herself in the bathtub. She had suffered for many years from recurrent depression and felt she had become "a burden" to herself and her family.

Chapter IV

Motivation

THE majority of suicide attempters have had long histories of psychiatric and social problems which often intensify prior to an attempt. The attempt itself does not result from a rational decision based on the assessment of a disrupted life experience. More often, an emotional state alters the individual's ability to correctly assess his or her situation, and leads to a tendency to overrespond to it. Suicide attempts often occur after a progressive build-up of tension and distortion of rational thought over a period of time that ranges from several minutes to several hours. In many instances, suicidal intent is negligible and the attempt results from a catastrophic sense of panic, tension, and confusion. In such a crisis, individuals momentarily lose their ability to utilize past adaptive habits. This pattern occurs more commonly than does careful planning of behavior. Alcohol may potentiate catastrophic reactions by further disrupting habitual adaptive responses, altering time perspective, and releasing uncontrollable emotional drives.

Seriousness of intent cannot be judged by the seriousness of the suicide act. Some patients have little control over their behavior and little awareness of their actions. Similarly, seriousness of intent cannot be minimized merely because others intervene.

Over half the patients studied were judged as nonserious. Several had no intent to injure themselves. A small percentage invariably are accidental. Forty-five percent of our patients made more serious attempts with considerable risk to their lives. These ranged in severity from ingestion of sufficient pills to produce coma to gunshot wounds. There does not seem to be a relationship between diagnosis and the seriousness of the act. Scores of severity of the attempt are based on a combined score of seriousness of intent and dangerousness of the act.

SERIOUSNESS

The life-threatening nature of the suicide attempt has been a major parameter in characterizing the motivation of suicide. Use of this criterion has, however, led to the undertreatment of patients who have made nondangerous attempts.

Most people accept as a valid explanation of suicide a wide range of rationalizations and fantasies concerning life after death, joining departed loved ones or ancestors. Attention to these highly idiosyncratic explanations has tended to obscure the obvious fact reported by almost all patients that their attempt occurred as part of an effort to gain relief from distressing tension, anxiety, and guilt, or from continued suffering.

The patient's behavior is at times a more valid index of motivation than the patient's own account, which may be distorted by denial and lack of awareness. The association of suicide attempts and interpersonal conflict has led many to stress the communicative or manipulative function of suicide behavior. Such comprehensible explanations, however, often foster the incorrect assumption that such attempts are less valid than the incomprehensible attempts of more disturbed patients.

Individuals with personality problems and interpersonal conflicts may be judged to be less suicidal because of their ability to communicate, their better level of general functioning, their higher reality testing, and the greater likelihood that the investigator will identify with them. In fact, the patient's behavior and motivational patterns relate to his psychological state more than to the seriousness or intent of the act.

An attempt is sometimes a conscious effort to *express anger and resentment toward others*. Others attempt suicide in an effort to live up to their threats. As one patient said: "I told everyone I would do it, so I had to do it." This pattern occurred most often where significant friends and relatives minimized the seriousness of the patient's distress, inducing conflict and the urge to act in the patient.

Oftentimes patients made weak attempts to get help, but were not explicit about their desires and were put off by others. It was almost as if they had set themselves up for rejection in order to get confirmation about their unworthiness.

Often the crisis has provided the patient with the opportunity to really level with loved ones who may have unwittingly been setting up excessively high standards.

"I started crying and I couldn't stop crying. I called my father and it seemed when I called my father that he was the one that I had wanted to call all the time, and he was the only one who responded. Of course, I was in tears when I called him and I really scared him. What they say is that they always thought that I was so strong that they didn't have to help me. I really don't know because I've been so weak that I don't know why they think I'm so strong, but I have always been very independent, not really, just seemingly. Kind of like, well, 'Don't you tell me what to do.' They say that when I was a little boy, they had no worries about me."

Rejection is often associated with an unwillingness of others to accept the patient's faults in such a way that they generate excessive guilt in him. Patients experience this as lack of concern or as proof others don't take them seriously.

"It's hard to believe that I am really serious about anything. I'm so emotional. God knows I'm like a *Symphonie Fantastique,* but it comes out all different, so that when I face people, they don't believe me. They are so used to my doing crazy things by now that anything I do is sort of, 'Oh, he's doing that again.' I really have to do something pretty wonderful now to prove to them that I'm really not out of my gourd.

"They form opinions, but they don't look at you to see if their opinions are right or not. They formed the opinion that I was a stable character, and they didn't pay attention to anything else. So many crazy things have happened to me this summer."

Sometimes a feeling of rejection is quite justified, since in their effort to help the patient, families actually criticize or ridicule. Responses vary with the social significance of the symptom, i.e., whether or not it was disturbing or strange.

"Well, he used to curse around the house, but later on, he was constantly talking to himself. At night, he would go into his room and you would hear him talking to himself, and you would go in and say, 'What's the matter?' and he would start complaining.

"We would get a little bit angry with him because we thought he was looking for sympathy and that he could stop complaining if he really wanted to. It suddenly hit me the last weekend I was home that he really couldn't stop it. We thought if we talked him out of it, you know, 'What do you have to worry about, these problems are so tiny,' but to him they were very important."

At times, suicide attempts result from the emotional "shakeup" or "regression" of a vulnerable individual that prevents him from relying on habitual responses and renders him susceptible to environmental influences.

Unlike religious and political conversion, where positive and integrative beliefs are introduced to the individual in a vulnerable or "regressive" emotional state, the susceptible patient may receive nothing but negative reinforcement, which further intensifies his or her helplessness and desperation. This is particularly true where the patient's symptoms are viewed as evidence of malevolence or manipulation.

DEGREE OF INTENT OF SUICIDE

Some patients attempt suicide with the knowledge that they will not be interrupted by relatives or friends. Others make indirect efforts to call attention to their behavior by taking pills in the presence of others. Some regret their actions immediately and call for help.

It is amazing how often a person accidentally returns home to discover a sleeping patient who cannot be awakened. Suicidal intent cannot be assessed in such instances. Occasionally, patients discovered in the act of suicide deny their actions. Without previous experience in assessing such situations, friends are often incapable of judging what has happened until the patient becomes increasingly confused, delirious, or somnolent, or makes a drastic effort to swallow another handful of pills, or makes a dash for the balcony. Efforts to mask an attempt sometimes lead to strange or bizarre behavior that the unwitting friend or relative fails to comprehend.

Once in the hospital, a small percentage of patients refuse to cooperate. They pull out intravenous infusions, refuse to eat, or make an effort to escape.

The multifaceted features of suicidal behavior make it difficult to assess the phenomenon of scare. The ingestion of a nonlethal amount of poison may be considered a gesture even when the patient expresses serious suicidal intentions. Where the act results in danger to life, the patient will be regarded as a serious risk, even if he denies intent.

One must differentiate between the dangerousness of an attempt and the seriousness of the patient's intent. To distinguish degrees of suicidal intent, one must assume that a death drive does not, in fact, occur in pure form, but instead results from a basic tension or ambivalence between the wish to live and the wish to die, so that one can recognize even minimal intent, which may be balanced by a much stronger wish to live.

Thus, whether an attempted suicide is dangerous or not, one can estimate the overall seriousness of intent by considering the patient's knowledge of the harmfulness of the drug ingested, his expressed desire to harm himself, and efforts made to obtain help after the attempt.

Suicide intent of a minimal degree may be said to exist where the patient knows that the amount of substance ingested is not lethal, although he intends to harm himself, and makes efforts to obtain help either by making the attempt in the presence of others or by immediately notifying others so as to guarantee prompt and effective attention.

Occasionally, this backfires and the anticipated help is not forthcoming. If this happens and the patient has not taken a lethal dose, no problems develop. However, if the assistance of others is left to chance factors—as when someone must cross town during rush hour, or cannot be located and the dose taken is known to be excessive—then the suicidal intent must be rated as severe.

Clearly, the most severe cases occur when a deadly

quantity of substance is taken with full knowledge of the consequences and where efforts are made to prevent others from helping. These are not difficult to identify. However, even in those cases, one occasionally encounters a patient who denies any intent.

From a clinical viewpoint, we evaluate the circumstances surrounding the attempt, the prior history of the patient, the state of consciousness at the time of the attempt, a recent history of illness, and the characteristics of the attempt itself. In this way, we try to assess whether or not the patient was, in fact, making a suicide attempt.

One patient left a note, took a near lethal dose of Doriden and on recovery, denied any attempt at suicide. He stated that he merely intended to sleep with two sleeping pills and that it was probably an accident that landed him in the hospital. His account was contradicted by the facts and by the story related to us by his family.

Attempts with more lethal methods may result from more serious intentions or from the availability of alternative means. One cannot simply conclude that those who make more active attempts are more suicidal than those who use passive methods, since the method chosen does not always relate to the intensity of the wish to die. In fact, it more often relates to personality factors.

Distinguishing attempts in terms of the consequences or dangerousness of the act also is not an accurate representation of reality. Many severely depressed patients intent on committing suicide are prevented from doing so or are accidentally discovered before harm occurs. They are still highly suicidal, even though they are likely to be rated as low risks.

There are many instances where agitated patients are stopped before leaping from a window. These people certainly do not suffer any physical effects and, indeed, are usually considered not suicidal. It is difficult to assess their intention, especially when this attempt is judged in terms of dangerousness. These patients frequently deny suicidal desires, emphasizing their momentary impulsive need to reduce tension.

One wonders whether those patients who die from jumping suffered from similar acute tension, which might have been controlled. There is too great an inclination to assume that completed suicide by jumping was a carefully premeditated act.

Talking to people who have survived an attempted suicide suggests that many completed suicides are accidental. These findings certainly emphasize the importance of the type of methods available. Where lethal methods are readily available, the suicide attempts are more likely to lead to death.

It is of interest that many patients who make serious suicide attempts subsequently insist that they did not wish to die. In our study of 300 patients, 27 percent wanted to let others know of their distress; 7 percent wanted "to get away"; 6.7 percent admitted that their attempt was merely a "scare tactic" to influence others; while 7.3 percent described their behavior as accidental. The high incidence of such explanations corresponds to the impulsive character of attempts. Most attempts are not planned but develop as emotional outbursts.

REASON FOR ATTEMPT

Patients cite distressing symptoms most often as the explanation for attempted suicide. Interpersonal conflict is the next most common explanation. Less frequently patients attribute their attempt to physical illness, loss of a loved one by death, major life changes, and confusion caused by drugs or alcohol.

Explanations for suicidal behavior most often relate to life situations. Young people generally blame interpersonal conflict for their attempts, while older people tend to select out factors more common in their experience, such as physical illness, death of a loved one, and advanced years.

One rarely finds a single motivational theme in a suicide attempt. Several motives often operate simultaneously or sequentially in the course of the act itself.

John K. began to cut his wrists when carbon monoxide inhalation failed to affect him. The sight of blood frightened him, as did his fear that, if he failed, his hand might be injured. A year later, he turned back from a window ledge, for fear that he might survive a jump as a cripple. One year later, he jumped in front of a speeding subway train and was killed instantly.

Another patient approached a window to jump, panicked, went to the bathroom, grabbed a razor, and cut her wrist. The blood scared her, and she called for help. Had she jumped, she could not have called for help.

The perceived absence of alternatives plays a crucial role in the suicide act. Once an individual initiates a suicidal act, he has redefined himself and opened the possibility of discovering new options. Thus, in many people, the motivation changes after the suicide act has begun.

A mood of tranquility sometimes occurs after the decision is made, as if the very act of setting a goal brings peace of mind. At that moment, the drive and tension are reduced, and the individual may change his or her mind. As one patient reported: "Problems cause a great deal of anxiety, a great deal of tension—physical and mental tension—which takes a lot of energy and is exhausting and keeps on being exhausting; and life gets very burdensome, and then the thought, the idea, of tranquility, or nonexistence, sounds very appealing. It is very relevant."

It is likely that many completed suicides occur because the victims chose irreversible methods that do not allow for a change of mind that might have shifted the course of action. The choice of methods depends on availability, timing, and also chance factors, and these are often unrelated to the seriousness of the suicidal intent.

Investigators generalizing from the experiences of such patients have emphasized the powerful motivating force of isolation and the absence of interpersonal ties. Observations of hysterical patients have led to generalizations about motivation which are often misapplied to patients with different personalities. This may lead to failure to recognize the early warning signs of suicidal behavior in patients who do not manifest evidence of what are considered the fundamental patterns of suicide.

The communication of distress to others has often been emphasized as a major determinant of suicidal behavior. This is frequently associated with other motives such as desire to retaliate for injured feelings, to provoke guilt in others, or to gain attention and affection. Patients motivated to do this are not necessarily intent on suicide, but are able to call attention to their distress by this behavior, thereby changing the attitudes of significant others.

Insofar as the consequences of suicide attempts are predictable, they are, to some extent, motivationally operative prior to the attempt, even when they occur at an unconscious level.

Suicidal behavior, like accidents and serious illness, may evoke sympathetic responses from others, which has led some to suggest that an "appeal for help" is another unconscious determinant of suicidal behavior. The cry for help most often results from interpersonal conflicts. Here, the attempt has value for its communicative impact on others. There is a manipulative element in such attempts as well as magical expectations that it may produce a significant change in relationships with others.

One young woman noted: "My emotions are governed by people. I'm susceptible to what people tell me. I'm so weak and that's my problem. I know exactly what's wrong with me and why, but emotionally how do you react? But finally, all these lies; the guy tells lies. And I don't know if they're pathological or if he's just got his own hang-ups. And finally, the whole thing just hit me, 'You're in with a bad guy' and I finally saw it. I feel very sorry for the guy. I went to him before when we were involved. But I couldn't work with him, he kept me in a constant emotional turmoil, like he knew Judy upset me, he knew that I felt horrible about taking him away from Judy, which is ridiculous to begin with, and so every now and then he made sure Judy was around.

"I'm very paranoiac. Very afraid of people. It depends on the people. I do my own thing, but if I get involved with a guy, all of a sudden, I don't know what to do. 'Cause my father was the kind of man who was very dominating, and all my life I always wanted to live up to my father, and I carry this need for a father image. I need somebody to protect me and take care of me, but I lose my identity too much. I become unsure of myself. I can't figure out why they dig me to begin with, and it's unfathomable to me that somebody could love me.

"I can't imagine anyone loving me. I can't see what there is to love, and there's nothing in the world that I want more than love, and that's why I took the pills. I said some of it was for spite, about my family.

"Almost everyone thinks about suicide at one point in their life; most people dismiss it. Even if you have a healthy ego, you have problems. See, that's what I want to be like myself, but life is a series of ups and downs. I realize that, but I'm still scared to death of life. Like last night. I was with my girl friend, and she was saying in a year and a half I should have myself out of debt, go to Europe, and this and that. I said, 'Boy, that would be great.' And I thought to myself, 'That will never happen to you.' I'm afraid if anything good ever does happen, it's going to be taken away. Like with my music, when something good happens, I've had people tell me that I was talented, and the man who wants to handle me is a very beautiful person. But I keep thinking about what I will do to make things go wrong.

"I took the pills because I was angry and filled with despair. I didn't take them with the intention of killing myself. Just a cry for help. And the only thing I got out of almost dying is, I thought, 'Wow, God must think I'm not really so bad because I should have died.' "

Personality patterns obviously play a role in influencing the individual's approach to suicide. Some people attempt suicide in a characteristically indecisive and ambivalent way. Such individuals may use a lethal method of suicide and simultaneously ensure the likelihood of their discovery. Others may leave the outcome to chance, as in Russian roulette where the outcome is left to God or fate.

An active, aggressive-decisive, assertive individual, by contrast, is more likely to utilize definitively lethal methods such as firearms, leaving little to chance. This does not necessarily mean that his suicidal drive is "more genuine" or "more serious," but rather it reflects his characteristic way of acting.

The ambivalent person abdicates responsibility for himself, leaving the results of his suicidal behavior to chance. Here a gambling instinct is at work. Here, the hope is that a suicide attempt will relieve depression or alter circumstances. The suicidal act itself may reflect this ambivalence.

As one young man noted: "It just sort of came into my head to do it. When it happened, I really wasn't conscious of what I was doing. I just sort of did it. I just gulped the pills down. There was no plan as to why I was doing this. I just wanted to do something self-destructive, and I thought that would work. I wasn't thinking that I would kill myself.

"I realized that I didn't *want* to be alive. We had all

been talking about the fact that if you want to be happy, you can, you know, if you just let yourself be. My friend is a clinical psychologist. He had been showing us that if you really want to be happy, you can, but one thing you don't do is dwell on your unhappiness. My brother told me once that he had been really unhappy and he just tried laughing. He got hysterical and he felt great. And he never did it again. He realized that he was really forcing himself to be unhappy.

"I don't know whether this was true, but I started thinking about the fact that I really didn't want to be either happy or unhappy. I just didn't want *to be* at all. I just went into the store and bought a handful of these, and I started crying, and I couldn't stop crying. Before I did this, I first called my analyst and asked to talk to somebody. I had to speak to somebody then."

Many believe that only a fine line separates the ambivalent attempter from the person with serious intentions. The girl friend of a patient who subsequently killed himself during his third suicide attempt noted, "And I just wonder if somebody gets it in his mind that he'll be wily about it. They try to hide it from people they know will try to stop them. They wait until they can do it. I think that's when the balance leaves because I think the first time Joe did it and even the second time, the will to live was balanced with the will to die, and the desire to live and the desire to die were both there, and they were both fighting.

"I have a feeling that when it gets to this point, the desire to live has become so suppressed, it's no longer a part of a person; it's just a desire to end it all. I really didn't think he'd do it."

Intense psychological discomfort characterizes the mental state of the suicide attempter. Patients report feelings of being overwhelmed with distressing emotions and a conviction that there is no hope of feeling better. Some, however, report minimal discomfort and occasionally people attempt suicide without conscious awareness.

Social pressure and general inexperience in handling feelings of anxiety and depression intensify the intolerance of discomfort, creating a psychological set in which impulsivity emerges.

The majority of suicide attempts are not premeditated, but occur impulsively in association with great psychological distress, stressful life circumstances, low frustration tolerance, interpersonal conflict, and alcohol and drug abuse.

Patients with lifelong histories of impulsive behavior, facilitated by alcohol excess and triggered by minor slights or arguments, are particularly risky. They make repeated attempts with little warning and in the face of slight stresses.

The nature of the suicide act cannot be isolated from the nature of the patient's personality and characteristic way of doing things. As such, it does not always have special significance or meaning, nor can one make special inferences about suicidal motivation on the basis of the act or the patient's communications.

Two case histories will illustrate some of these points. Barbara K., a 42-year-old woman with a history of heavy drinking for years, a complicated and unsatisfactory set of life circumstances, e.g., her children live with her former husband and a fiancé broke up with her because of her heavy drinking. She doesn't work because she doesn't want to do menial tasks, and she has enough money to support a private summer house.

At 4:15 P.M., she said to her lover that she would kill herself. She had had a pint. She doesn't remember taking the razor and cutting her wrist, but then she called a friend and was taken to the hospital. She didn't want to die; she was not angry with herself and never gets depressed. This patient exhibited a not uncommon pattern of impulsivity associated with heavy alcohol consumption and the cessation of a gratifying dependency relationship. These precipitated a temper tantrum, outburst, or irrational generalized rage directed at no one in particular.

The duration of the suicidal impulse was brief and did not give rise to much concern, thought, doubt, or preparation. The act was equally brief and was followed by little distress, remorse, or concern for its effects on others.

An explanation for the brevity of the suicidal impulse and the suicidal act may reasonably be sought in both the impulsive superficial nature of this woman's personality and her characteristic way of handling stress in an unorganized and ineffective manner. She might easily have been persuaded out of this if she had been given a slight bit of support at the time of the attempt.

Barbara K. is to be contrasted with Betty S., who made a serious attempt, lacerating nerves, tendons, and arteries, which produced a state of shock and prevented her from calling for help.

Two features stand out here. One is the fact that having gone to the window to jump, the patient stopped because she didn't want to die. Then she started crying, fixed another drink, took two Miltowns and went into the bathroom "to find something to do." She was tense. She saw a razor, picked it up, and the next thing she knew, her arm was bleeding. She doesn't remember a suicidal thought at the time she actually lacerated herself. Immediately, she thought of getting help, but was weakened by shock. The suicidal act occurred in what appears to have been an altered state of consciousness without the organization and clarity of purpose that, in retrospect, she feels would be the way she would have done it if she really wanted to do it right.

It is also of interest to consider that she may have been pushed into this impulsive state by her therapist's overconcern. She called him before leaving her boy friend's house, and he insisted on seeing her. He offered to have coffee with her later or when she called him from her house.

He also relayed messages from her boy friend to her. He also discovered her body after he went to her house.

One can only speculate as to the nature of his involvement in terms of his feelings of guilt, concern, and responsibility, but his participation suggests that he may have kept her in distress by continually trying to be reassured by her that everything was all right. How much this was an expression of his dependency, further reducing her strength and the satisfaction of her own dependency needs, is hard to say. The interested, overconcerned help given may, however, anger the patients who cannot express it because they want to be reassured themselves. This reduces the patient to infantilism and simultaneously he or she demands absolution from others. This produces tremendous conflict and guilt in the patient, and perhaps great confusion, and a genuine desire to be left alone. Suicide may be the only escape.

L.T. wrote two notes before her first suicide attempt and one after swallowing the pills, instructing the family on the disposal of her body. The first letter was a note to her husband and daughter about her possessions, and an explanation of her reasons for suicide:

"I'm very, very sorry. I love you both, but I guess not enough to want to live. This whole illness business has been just too much. . . . Good-bye to both of you and God be with you, as He wasn't with me."

A second note to her doctor was more revealing:

"Thanks for nothing. You are cruel and you can slay a person—a *sensitive* person—with one word. And I was sensitive and, therefore, vulnerable."

The third note was scrawled in bold letters after the pills were beginning to work in her system. "I'm tired of begging for help! 1. Burial as quick as possible; 2. no open casket; 3. no embalming, if possible."

In general, few patients are calm prior to an attempt. Most experienced much discomfort for a considerable time beforehand.

Chapter V

Drug and Alcohol Abuse

THE use of alcohol is a common accompaniment of suicidal behavior. Alcohol serves to reduce inhibitions and enables the individual to act out his or her fantasies. It also serves to create additional depression.

Complex combinations of physical, biochemical, psychological, and social factors make certain individuals susceptible to alcohol problems under certain conditions. Alcohol, widely available in the workaday world, can rapidly alleviate symptoms of anxiety and depression leaving little impetus to develop constructive measures for reducing stress or alleviating anxiety. The utilization of adaptive skills is bypassed by this route to temporary relief, which in the end may actually intensify the symptoms and increase the demand for more alcohol.

ALCOHOL ABUSE

Problem drinking produces many effects in the friends and relatives of the alcoholic. These effects range from helpful responses that can speed the alcoholic's efforts to seek help, to fear and anger, which complicate the drinker's difficulties. The discovery of problem drinking can induce fear of such magnitude that friends and relatives may accept the myth that the alcoholic is incurable and that he is hell-bent for skid row, the breakup of his family, and various crippling, degenerative physical processes. These negative responses may intensify, not diminish, the drinking. Unsuccessful efforts to stop drinking may reinforce these pessimistic expectations.

The use of alcohol is reinforced by its obvious effects and people are able to tolerate larger quantities in time. Gradually, either normal functioning requires bolstering with alcohol, or symptoms of withdrawal occur with the cessation of drinking. The reduction of fear associated with these experiences provides additional reinforcement of the alcohol habit.

It is sometimes necessary for serious problems to develop before the individual recognizes his drinking excesses.

There are certain characteristic problems likely to be experienced by alcoholics. These generally relate to dependency and fear of authority, and power struggles. Often, alcoholic or prealcoholic individuals may confuse their objectives with an organization's or may feel the need to conform to role expectations.

The individual may be responsible for supervising the work of others and this may conflict with his own inclination to depend on others and to be liked by them, which inhibits him from being firm or critical as necessary. These conflicts obviously relate more to the management of people than to the technical requirements of the job.

Increased work pressure from a demanding boss may also frustrate the individual's need for approval, reduce his confidence, and intensify his need to drink. A variety of interpersonal situations that create anxiety foster excessive alcohol consumption. Sometimes, however, excessive drinking results simply from habitual use on business or social occasions, where alcohol acts as a social catalyst or lubricant, and the refusal to drink is an indication of "bad manners." A diagnosis of alcoholism is generally not made until it has progressed to serious proportions. As such, appropriate treatment is not provided often at the time when it might do the most good.

The social acceptance of drinking, the fact that a person may continue to function on his job and rarely appear intoxicated, fosters an even worse response—denial of the problem. These rationalizations fail to take into consideration the fact that as the individual increases his intake, he is likely to appear less intoxicated. But he may have become dependent on the alcohol and will experience dreadful tension and anxiety states should he not have it to sustain him in coping with the ordinary stresses of daily life.

While the early manifestations of alcoholism include such alterations of function as loss of efficiency, loss of initiative, a decline in the ability to concentrate, and altered judgment, the enormous amount of social drinking that everyone engages in makes it possible for the prealcoholic to continue to appear to be functioning without anyone noticing the declining performance.

The stresses built into the workaday world relate to shifts in individual responsibility, shifts from professional to administrative roles, retirement, transfers, and interpersonal conflicts affording the individual environmental explanations for the distress, serving, therefore, to disguise an alcohol problem.

The heavy use of alcohol as a social catalyst in the business world also makes it difficult to differentiate the occasional social drinker from the regular social drinker, who may become habituated to alcohol unwittingly.

While some individuals with alcohol problems may be able to limit their drinking, most cannot. Therefore, total abstinence based on inability to handle alcohol is recommended.

Alcohol contributes to suicidal tendencies by reducing the capacity to cope with problems, by causing depressive symptomatology, by undermining confidence, and by weakening defenses. Withdrawal symptoms for those who drink excessively may generate intolerable tension and provoke hostility from others, further reinforcing a negative self-image.

While alcohol may reduce tension, anxiety, and depression in some people, for others, particularly the acutely disturbed, the alcohol, acting in combination with barbiturates, tension, depression, and acute stress, increases the suicidal drive by increasing confusion, and reducing the inhibition against self-destructive behavior.

Inability to control alcohol intake, coupled with extra pressure that increases the "need" for alcohol, initiates a vicious circle. The patient must modify his behavior to correct for his inability to function under the influence of alcohol. He may try to cover up his drinking. He may drink in anticipation of uncomfortable situations to prevent tension. Eventually, the alcohol impairs ability to cope, further intensifying the problem. Withdrawal from activities follows.

A crisis state begins in such patients with the onset of severe tension and anxiety frequently precipitated by a real or feared threat to their security; this condition is initially relieved by alcohol. However, the consumption of a large amount of alcohol weakens ego defenses and causes flooding thoughts and memories of childhood and an intensification of suicidal ideation. The prognosis for such patients is guarded because they rarely accept their alcoholic status and resist seeking supportive help.

Instituting a substitute behavior at times of stress is

also difficult because when these individuals do not drink, they usually are symptom-free, and function well.

"I was released from Manhattan State Hospital in June after a breakdown, was put on welfare and into a welfare hotel alone. I had been living on the East Side previously and began to drink heavily and take pills. I tried to work, but was fired for being high at work. Two weeks ago, I took a knife and started to stab myself but I couldn't because I didn't want to feel the pain. If I'd had thirty seconds, I would have swallowed all the pills.

"I came out of a hospital into that environment and was also living alone. I can't seem to grow up. Losing my job was the last straw. Then I really began to destroy myself.

"When I left my boy friend and returned to my daughter, things were all right for awhile. Then I decided I didn't want my daughter and wanted to return to him, but couldn't. I began taking pills and wound up in Manhattan State.

"I have very little desire to keep going. I can't sleep and drink as much as I can get. I can't eat sometimes going on four to five days. Suicide keeps coming into my thoughts.

"I have not been able to care for my child since my divorce. I've hurt my mother in many ways by failing to get back on my feet."

Alcoholism impinges on friends and relatives, some of whom suffer from the alcoholic's insensitivity, unpredictability, and unreliability. Mrs. Elizabeth K. described the following:

"My husband is an alcoholic and I realize this is an illness, but he doesn't think that he has anything at all to do with my getting ill. But I know he has. It seems I can take it up to a certain point, and then I just seem to go to pieces. He always reminds me that I was sick a very long time ago, even before he met me, which is true, but he's not helping any by calling me all sorts of names and not cooperating by helping himself. There are times when I cook and wait and wait but he does not come home until very late.

"I got very discouraged about my husband's not stopping his drinking. I thought to myself, he will never change, so what's the use of trying to reach him. He always claims he has nothing to do with my getting sick, but I certainly feel that he has. If he would only realize how he hurts me by being so inconsiderate, I am sure he would try to change."

It is difficult to differentiate between pathological and normal drinking patterns. An individual may suffer from early alcoholism without evidence of intoxication. Alcoholism does not necessarily relate to the amount of alcohol used. To the extent that loss of control, secondary to alcohol, may occur without evidence of intoxication, the behavior may be incorrectly attributed to personality or situational factors rather than to the alcohol. Alcohol may also impair memory about disturbing events and reduce the incentive for modification of the drinking pattern. Difficulty in recognition of alcoholism is also due to the fact that there is no single personality type that is predisposed to alcoholism.

To the extent that alcoholism develops from a variety of complex factors, it is often difficult to label an individual's problem as such, especially when he or she does not display any evidence of malfunctioning or maladaptation. Thus people who drink more than is considered normal or who drink to the point that they think about their use of alcohol may not be recognized as alcoholics.

In fact, these underlying patterns of behavior are more often than not evidence of grossly abnormal, intoxicated, or deviant behavior secondary to alcohol. Many individuals drink excessively to relieve depressive symptoms, feelings of inadequacy, or other difficulties.

Another pattern relates to the circular nature of alcohol usage in such a way that guilt and anxiety over alcohol abuse lead to increased alcohol consumption, progressive decline of general functioning, and the risk of physiological addiction. The alcohol problems of this group often go unrecognized despite the fact that these people are more likely to seek help. Chafetz (1965) has labeled them "reactive alcoholics," to be distinguished from the "addictive alcoholics," who are more often recognized as alcoholic.

The first group corresponds to Jellenek's (1960) category of alpha alcoholics. The second (whose characteristic behavior conforms to the conventional stereotype of alcoholics) corresponds to Jellenek's "gamma type," who have demonstrable physiological changes and neurological and physical organ damage as a result of their alcohol intake and dietary deficiencies. While the "gamma type" clearly require medical treatment, the alpha type can generally be handled by counseling.

A history of early opportunities to identify with a parent or significant other person who has a drinking problem, or experience in a sociocultural setting with permissive attitudes toward alcohol, are among the most important predisposing factors.

A detailed review of the situations usually associated with drinking may reveal to the individual subtle interpersonal pressures inducing him to drink, and may help him design a series of sensible strategies to confine his drinking to specified situations and fixed, limited amounts. The object here is to assist the individual to gain control over his drinking by designating specific times and places to drink— consciously deciding to do so rather than doing it solely on a reactive basis ultimately with the hope of gaining the power of control over the drinking pattern.

Preaching and moralizing about the harmfulness of alcohol frequently induces guilt, which may precipitate more drinking. Supportive attitudes are more effective.

DRUG ABUSE

To a considerable extent, drug abuse is associated with the drug subculture among adolescents and young adults. This subculture has built into it a large element of self-destructive behavior associated with the abuse of a variety of potent pharmacological sedatives, stimulants, and hallucinogens.

Acting out, defiance of authority, and submission to peer-group pressures are distinguishable characteristics of this culture. For "borderline" personality types, the group pressures combined with the drug effects may produce regressive behavior and a loss of self-control, leading at times to serious behavioral disturbances, which may be rationalized as a search for new values, a new identity, and a meaningful life.

Parents and those in authority may respond only to the "deviant" aspects of this behavior, failing to recognize the self-medicating dimension of it. Nonrecognition of the underlying illness may produce complications; often overdoses of "hard" and "soft" drugs result from individual efforts to gain greater relief or from a loss of control and confusion associated with the use of excessive quantities. At times, drug use unleashes depressive symptoms that become overwhelming, prompting individuals to attempt "to sleep" indefinitely to eliminate the distress.

Many young patients turn to marijuana, LSD, methedrine, and heroin for the relief of distressing symptoms or for the integrative experience they anticipate from such psychoactive agents. The resulting altered states of consciousness often produce loss of contact and a reduction in the ability to cope with stress situations.

Patients on "speed" often become paranoid and hyperactive, while those who use LSD report schizophreniclike experiences and loss of the ties that normally bind them to reality. Efforts to find a positive integrative experience may be frustrated, and patients may become increasingly susceptible to environmental stress with a resulting increase in suicidal drive. The following remarks illustrate the nature of this loss of reality testing ability under the influence of drugs.

"Like I was afraid, and I didn't want to be under everybody's control. I didn't want that, but when I was tripping it was bad, like I couldn't get to him, and I went to someone else, not sexually. I'm just talking about my head when I'm confused. I don't know exactly what it is, but you can't get onto the trend of thought. Your mind goes nuts. It's like you don't know where to place your head, so to speak. You don't know what direction to put it in and if you put it there, you're not satisfied, and you don't know what you want, and you get crazy from it.

"See, he couldn't relax and try to lose his ego with it, 'cause he was too worried about what my state of mind was. He was able just to go along with it, but I just couldn't. Then you get to the point where your head is getting nuts. You take it off, and you put on music and then you can't hear any other music but that music and that'll drive you crazy. You become the people that are in the opera. You're acting a part even if it's in German or French or whatever it is. You know what's happening."

⌐ The loss of ego control and body boundaries is another manifestation of drug use. "You hear the sound so you become part of that sound. No, I was looking at my hand or my foot and one time I took a half, and four hours later, it was like I was there, but I wasn't there, and I wanted the other half so he took the other half with me and each component that makes up acid has different effects on you, and I felt the heat of his body.

"I felt I was melting into him. It was just incredible. It's like I was liquid. And you become like one. You could feel the heat, and it was so intense. I never had that happen again. I wouldn't say everybody should try it, but I'm glad

I did. I wouldn't do it again because I'm scared that it's too damaging."

These reactions increase the risk of paranoid reactions: "People take LSD and then they go in the street and that's when you catch the horrors 'cause you're so paranoid that you get nuts with it and people don't know you're under acid. A friend of mine did it a lot, and she said it's around the one hundred and fifth trip that you start seeing things in yourself that you don't like. Everybody has these things but can't accept them. They're real horrible. And I guess because they're so intensified that you can't face them. LSD takes everything out of proportion.

"The danger of LSD is that you're seeing things that are interpreted as being valid and then you subsequently act on it. The significant thing with LSD or any of these mind-altering drugs that alter consciousness is the impact of the situation and the meaning of the situation, so that your kind of sensitivity is not getting in with somebody that's going to exploit you. That's really the essence of it. It's an ideal situation for introducing new ideas, new ideologies, and the like."

Now, often the people involved with LSD have their own problems and can't provide the necessary support to others. They, too, want to be reassured but don't have good coping methods and thus, acting by habit, they over-involve themselves in the panic of others. These pressures sometimes operate outside the LSD context.

Patty R. said: "I have a friend. It was maybe a week before I came here and she's telling me all these things and she made me feel like I was on acid again. My head got so confused that I didn't know where to put it. I got so crazy I was pacing. I didn't know what to do with myself. I kept wondering, 'What's her game?'"

The suicide potential of patients taking LSD is considerable because of the marked alteration in judgment, and the confusion and terrifying hallucinations that result.

Suicidal acts may occur in certain instances because of the patient's urgent need to escape the horrible subjective state experienced. The drug usage in and of itself may not be intentionally self-destructive. However, it serves to diminish the strength of habitual defenses, and indirectly contributes to the self-destructive outcome by weakening the individual's resistance to stresses, including those inherent in the social context of drug use. Drug abuse also provokes negative reactions from parents and significant others, which also adds to the individual's guilt and distress.

Chapter VI

Suicide
Potential

SUICIDE attempts rarely occur out of the blue.
There are clues preceding the attempt, which if
recognized, may increase the chances for the patients to
seek or obtain help. Characteristics of patients with potential
for suicide include a history of gesturing in response to interpersonal conflict. There may have been threats in the
heat of anger or at the peak of disappointment. No prior
plans. While at low risk, such gestures cannot but be minimized since they reflect a characteristic style of coping that
obviously has maladaptive features to it. A past history of
self-destructive behavior and/or violent acts toward others
also points to a potential for impulsive and violent acting
out, which may operate in a given individual under certain
stressful circumstances.

Suicide potential may be judged to be high if the patient reveals well thought out plans and a preoccupation
with a desire to die, is socially isolated, elderly, and de-

pressed. Delusional ideation about the necessity of death must also be considered a significant precursor, particularly if the patient has enough pills or other means to kill himself, is chronically depressed or schizophrenic, and has a history of a recent major attempt.

SUICIDAL FANTASIES

The frequency of suicidal calls to suicide-prevention centers reflects the widespread prevalence of suicidal thoughts. It may be that almost all people think of suicide or the desirability of "ending it all" at some time in the course of their lives. For some people, suicidal thoughts are distressing in and of themselves and are experienced as intrusive, strange, and uncontrollable. Thoughts of suicide are not, however, always frightening or distressing and often persist over time in depressed people as an "ace in the hole," a final option to be exposed when situations fail to materialize or they become overwhelming.

"There were always the razor blades. I had fantasies about how to do it. I would just have fantasies about taking an overdose of sleeping pills and turning the radio on and romantically fading away. Everybody would come in and discover my body. These thoughts were not scary. They were very pleasant as a matter of fact. I'd go out of my mind and go around in a daze and have everybody pat me on the head and say, 'Poor David.' I've had these kinds of thoughts ever since I was six years old."

Suicidal thoughts may be part of a long-standing pattern, and the attempt part of a cumulative history, each attempt bringing the individual closer to a more serious outcome.

"I remember after I had swallowed those pills this time. I started crying and I felt the way I had that last time in the summer. It was like a continuation of it, as if there had never been any time in between. I bought the pills, and

I lived with them a couple of months, and then I took them. It was like a continuation of something that I started a long time ago. I was finishing what I had started. Buying the pills is or was actually more painful than doing it. I never know when that is going to happen. I feel I am building up to something right now, confusion, new thoughts all the time, utter confusion."

THREATS

What significance should one attach to threats of suicide? Such threats should be taken seriously. To the extent that they evoke negativism and may be challenged in an effort to "call the patient's bluff" and stop the attempt, they represent a dramatic example of the boomerang effect.

One man described the following: "She was talking about killing herself and she locked herself in the bathroom. I told her this was weird, and that I didn't want to lose her. What was the purpose in it? And she locked herself up and she started to cry, and then she relaxed. I said, 'Go on and kill yourself and you'll be the biggest loser in the long run.' I went after her and she said she wouldn't.

"I didn't know what I should do, whether I should laugh or cry. I said, 'Just do it, just do it.' I thought she would relax after I repeated it so many times. I didn't understand it, you know, people who had this kind of trouble. I thought it was kind of funny that she would try to kill herself when she had so many things to live for. This was a stupid way to get rid of your problems. I didn't know how to handle the situation. What could I do? If I try to stop her, she would continue. When I left her, she was biting her hair . . . she cut her own hair. She cut the skin, but I don't think she took any scalp. You know, whenever she didn't have anything else to do, she cut her hands. She would hurt herself. I didn't call the doctor, because I thought it was just nerves. Frankly, I didn't understand the problem, but

I think I can understand now that she is unbalanced."

REPEATED ATTEMPTS

A history of a previous attempt is an important clue to suicide risk when other factors are present. There are, in fact, certain patients who make repeated attempts and who form a distinct clinical group. Their self-destructiveness reflects a learned behavioral pattern designed to attract attention, "punish" the patient, relieve tension, escape into sleep, avoid criticism, or serve some purpose other than actual suicide.

Repeated attempts often occur that are not associated with the intention to die. One patient believed in the medieval custom of blood-letting. Periodically, he lacerated his arm with a razor and watched the blood come out. This made him "feel better." He never thought of dying and did not intend to or want to die. While his lacerations were rarely severe, his risk was not minimal, since he was a social isolate. He was always in danger of accidentally harming himself and not being able to obtain help in time.

Some patients put themselves beyond help by inducing others to take firm stands and then resisting them, expressing resentment of the help. Restlessness and uncooperativeness also occur. Where such attitudes persist, the prognosis remains guarded since therapeutic efforts may at times provoke self-destructive responses.

The persistence of delusions that prompted an initial attempt is another common element in repeated attempts, particularly in cases where the severity of the psychotic disorder is not adequately recognized. One patient was depressed, "Because I had these eyes looking at me . . . a voice telling me I had to die. The voice told me to kill, but I couldn't." The hallucinatory pressure drove her to jump into the river with her baby. Rescued and hospitalized, she continued to believe that the devil's eyes were after her because "I didn't tell my doctor the truth." The persistence of these thoughts led to a second attempt in the hospital.

It is difficult to judge the risk in such patients whose thought processes are difficult to discern. It is easier to judge the risk of depressed patients.

Occasionally, repeated attempts occur shortly after the patient leaves an emergency room without provision for psychiatric follow-up. Repeated attempts usually resemble earlier attempts in terms of circumstances, method, and degree of danger. A return to the same noxious social situations triggers responses that evolve much like previous attempts.

Marital conflicts, unsatisfactory homosexual relationships, or business problems most commonly set off repeated attempts. Repetitive self-poisoning commonly occurs in barbiturate abusers, who frequently ingest progressively larger amounts of drugs to reduce tension or eliminate insomnia and who often accidentally ingest more than their systems can tolerate.

Self-mutilation with glass or razor blades rarely proves dangerous. Such behavior usually occurs during an irrational moment. One patient experienced "fits of rage" characterized by severe scratching of her body. Unaccompanied by pain, such "fits" seem to occur in a dissociative state of mind in which the patient is not fully cognizant of his or her actions. Medicine reduces the frequency and severity of such fits but does not eliminate them. Set off by minor frustrations, patients may scream and scratch themselves to the point of bleeding. When calm, they describe considerable fear of their inability to control their impulses because of the enormous tension behind this behavior.

Alcohol abuse reduces inhibitions of self-destructiveness and prevents modification of life situations. Alcohol alters consciousness, judgment, and the capacity to assess the significance and seriousness of impulsive drives and may magnify the dangerousness of a suicidal act. Alcohol potentiates the effect of other pills that the patient might have ingested.

Patients with multiple attempts often seem undisturbed between episodes and are sometimes judged as attention seekers, the seriousness of their genuine disturbance and suicide potential being ignored by friends, relatives, physicians, and sometimes hospital personnel. One thirty-year-old mechanic had arms and wrists scarred from eight attempts. He remembered the circumstances surrounding each episode and described his increasing skill at producing a deeper scar with a razor. Most episodes occurred while he was under the influence of alcohol, which he drank excessively when depressed. He described a progressive obsession with thoughts of the razor, slashing himself, seeing the blood gush out, and eventually dying. These obsessive thoughts were accompanied by compulsion to slash himself without any positive suicidal desires. Wrist cutting brought him relief of tension in contrast to others whose objective was the subsequent ordeal of pain and alleviation of guilt.

Chapter VII

Social and Environmental Stress

THE nature of stressful experiences relates to certain patient characteristics. Older patients tend to suffer from physical illnesses, isolation, separation, and widowhood to a greater extent than younger patients. Married patients suffered from more marital conflict and threats of separation than single patients.

OBJECTIVE STRESSES

Objectively stressful life circumstances occur in almost half the patients who attempt suicide. These objective stresses run the gamut from loss of a loved one to loss of a job. In assessing stress, it is useful to differentiate between objective stresses arising independently, and those resulting from the patient's behavior.

Clearly, the healthier individuals can tolerate more severe stress. More troubled patients can tolerate less. Quite clearly, conflict with others was the common denominator of most stresses reported by patients.

INTERPERSONAL CONFLICT

What kinds of interpersonal relationships exist? Are they supportive, noxious? Do they impede the patient's autonomy? Do they prove a threat to the patient's emotional well-being and physical safety?

Psychiatrists have long been aware that environmental factors can influence certain characteristics of psychiatric disorders. Social neglect accounts for the chronic deterioration and social disabilities of long-term patients treated in custodial institutions.

Similarly, suicidal behavior often results from failure of relatives and friends to recognize the patient's distress or handicaps and their resulting attribution of negative traits and attitudes to the patient. These imply that the patient is "searching for attention," "full of self-pity," and other derogatory labels that may contribute to the patient's loss of self-esteem and sense of hopelessness.

Patients often remain in what may be considered a chronic sick role long after symptoms of psychological illness have remitted. They may be protected and controlled as if they were helpless or potentially suicidal, a pattern of expectations that may, in fact, increase the suicide risk. The combination of stress and support creates ambivalence, as well as problems of reality testing, identity, and authority.

Ordinary life stresses are magnified in some patients, taking the form of suspicion of others, poor control over emotions, and a limited self-concept. Delusional thinking may lead a patient to retaliate against imagined wrongs. Retaliation by others may confirm the patient's suspicions. The inability to trust others whom the patient must rely upon creates stormy interpersonal relationships. Patients test the concern of others, especially kindness and support.

Efforts to be credited with "good" behavior and "progress" in therapy are often difficult to differentiate from mature assumptions of personal responsibility. The expression of satisfaction or increased expectations about the patient's potential for accomplishment often threatens the patient and leads to self-destructive behavior.

Depressed patients frequently discover the unwillingness of others to support their claims for help. Such rejection may intensify their guilt and sense of worthlessness. Stressful rejection undermines confidence, intensifies depressive symptoms, and often increases suicidal risk.

Symptoms also influence environmental responses. People who complain about declining energy and failures may anger others who cannot comprehend whining dependency and apparent stability in the same person and cannot tolerate their argumentativeness and unwillingness to accept advice. Power struggles may ensue and overwhelm patients even more.

Failure to maintain a sense of autonomy and excessive dependency are often at the root of interpersonal conflict. Such relationships discourage individual autonomy, encourage passive dependency, and make inflexible demands on each other in terms of unrealistic expectations of mutual support, which the individual is fearful of denying.

One patient and her husband shared their living quarters with another couple and gradually drifted toward an exchange of spouses. Their basic dependency and fear of rejection prevented them from setting limits on the relationship. Their life spaces were undefined and ambiguous and led progressively to sexual involvement of the patient with the other spouse, an acute sense of guilt, and a desperate suicide attempt, designed to stop the painfulness of her anxiety and guilt. Here, the patient was pushed into this unsatisfactory situation by her husband, who was clearly rejecting her this way. Inadequate or noxious social relationships may contribute to demoralization, a sense of worthlessness, and a conviction of the validity of suicide as a release from distress. Untenable relationships with married or otherwise attached men can prove stressful for young women eager to marry.

Married life generates numerous psychological conflicts as well. While the ability to live in a sustained marital relationship reflects the ability to have close personal relationships, marriage does lead to various stresses and conflicts relating to the responsibility of child-rearing and problems with in-laws.

The disruptive effects of divorce, separation, and widowhood differ at different times in the lives of individuals. Divorce at thirty-five may be more stressful than divorce at age twenty-one. To be widowed at twenty-one with two children may be less of a stress than to be widowed at an older age. The termination of relationships, the intensification of conflict and other associated factors affect people differently, depending on their age, sex, physical health, and other factors.

Threat of separation and of impending divorce commonly generates stress, particularly if an individual fails to recognize that he or she may have the potential to cope alone.

Marital conflict may be increased by external factors, such as illness and financial pressures. Illness in the family of husband and wife, which necessitates a return to the parental home, may result in exacerbation of lifelong conflicts. Contact with other family members may also intensify distress.

Neurotic factors may impair capacity to function in close relationships or may lead people to become involved in other destructive relationships. Emotional difficulties may become the focal issue of ridicule that may make the patient increasingly dependent upon a relative, who may unwittingly exploit the patient's sense of guilt and culpability.

Constant stress secondary to the alcohol or drug abuse of a spouse sometimes occurs. Often people remain in such situations because of a desire to dominate and/or to be considered to be martyrs. As such, they often prove to have a vested interest in the perpetuation of the very difficulties about which they complained. Efforts to change a spouse can produce conflict and precipitate a crisis.

Marital conflicts generally develop around questions of money, sex, relatives, children, and general values. Differences of opinion and varying degrees of tolerance for differences contribute to the conflict. Not the differences, but the unwillingness to tolerate differences creates friction, defensive-manipulative maneuvers, conflict, and crisis when the spouses cannot restore a reasonable balance.

Patients often seek extramarital liaisons to escape total domination, only to find themselves duplicating the same patterns, albeit in a diluted way, in these relationships. Mutual confession in sadomasochistic relationships serves to maintain conflict. Arguments stem from this, intensifying feelings of isolation.

Repetition, lack of intimacy, provocation of significant others characterize many of these relationships.

Melinda M. was in conflict with her boy friend and her parents, who opposed her unpredictable, inconsiderate, destructive, hostile, and promiscuous behavior. She dropped out of high school, defiantly took drugs to taunt her parents, posed nude for a photographer, and provoked a fight between her boy friend and another friend whom she accused of raping her.

Her impulsivity and self-indulgence were manifested by temper tantrums and marked jealousy of a younger sibling. Parental criticism and rejection further intensified her behavior. Her father branded her a "cheap bitch" and a "whore." Her mother feared she would "take to the streets" if too many controls were introduced. Seeking to prove her parents were right, she entered into many transitory relationships, which invariably failed because of her self-depreciative attitudes and demandingness. She continually found herself in vicious circles of excessive self-depreciation and guilt.

Another pattern characterized by continual criticism fosters negative expectations that the patient accepts unconsciously hoping to gain some perverted kind of approval.

Conflict often ensues when husband and wife come from backgrounds that differ in terms of the distribution of authority and the allocation of responsibility for decision-making. Conflict may arise over decisions about money, the discipline of children, the selection of residence, and the like. Attempts to involve children in the conflict add to the tension. It is difficult to develop new ways of relating since present patterns are quite automatic and difficult to recognize, as well as persistent because of their familiarity and sameness.

Modification involves changes in certain basic personality traits that are often essential to a self-concept, and which they are reluctant to change. Only when patients become actively engaged in pursuing a goal, can they begin to generate some of the will to genuinely realize some of their basic potential.

A tendency to act compliantly and to harbor resentment characterizes some patients. As one patient noted: "If something bothered me, I wouldn't say anything about it, and I would start to complain about something minor. I used to think I was frightfully popular. I used to want everyone to think I was nice and to like me. Now, I don't care."

This patient was dependent on her sister, whom she believed prettier than she was. The patient could never really express her feelings to her sister. Since then, they have had a big fight and cleared the air. "Right now, I think of us as individuals. I have to say what I want to say. If someone doesn't like me for it, then there wasn't much to our relationship anyway."

Some patients derive gratification and a reduction of

guilt from their suffering. Repeated suicidal behavior often enables the patient to dominate others without having to experience the rejection of direct requests to get others to change. In such passive-aggressive acts, the patient was able to arouse considerable guilt in others, while simultaneously appearing to be victimized.

Dependency needs are also satisfied by getting others to set limits. Such behavior also enables individuals to sustain unsatisfactory neurotic and pathological relationships despite their immature, demanding, and irresponsible ways. Suicidal behavior became a recurrent theme in some relationships characterized by conflict, hostility, jealousy, and other pathological emotions that reduced boredom and "brought their feelings to life." At times, when relationships are threatened by change, suicidal behavior serves to reestablish the old equilibrium. Conflict is often precipitated by an inclination to see withdrawal as personal rejection rather than manifestation of depression.

Some people with life stresses are unable to utilize appropriate defenses in dealing with them. They perceive problems unrealistically and fail to assess their own strengths. In a somewhat distorted way, their strength and self-assertiveness may be manifested in the suicidal act.

Self-pitying and alienated by depression, the suicide attempt may be an existential assertion of control, prompted by feelings that these individuals are no longer responsible to those who had rejected them and no longer have to act in terms of others' expectations. This "I don't give a damn what you think" attitude accounted for an ability to establish new relationships subsequent to the suicide attempt.

The attempt may put an individual beyond the ken of his usual obligations and give him renewed power over his destiny. This increase in personal freedom may account for the inclination of others to react negatively to the attempt as if it were deviant behavior. This increases suicidal risk.

Doctors, close friends, and relatives, and even the

patient have frequently failed to recognize the existence of illness and the fact that the patient's distress and inability to function were not willful and purposeful. Superficial cheerfulness and calm often mask underlying insecurity, low frustration tolerance, and inability to deal with stress and minor depressive symptoms.

Identity problems are often accompanied by defiance of authority. This may be manifested in drug abuse, sexual promiscuity, interpersonal conflicts, and occasionally verbal or physical assaultiveness. Nonresponsiveness on the part of authority figures intensifies guilt and anxiety and may lead to more defiant behavior until limits are set. Patients with identity problems can be particularly obstreperous in a hospital setting where they may ignore activities, refuse medicine, and demand privileges, thereby provoking the imposition of constraints.

Psychiatric disorders alter self-awareness and the ability to recognize the illness itself. Depression fosters pessimism, schizophrenia, a sense of terror, and distortion of perceptions that increase the patient's willingness to accept the negative evaluations of others.

Suicide becomes a risk as a result of a combination of psychiatric, personality, and environmental factors. The patient's adaptation to an illness and environmental stress may best be understood in terms of his previous experience and whether his personality defenses have been altered by age or the progressive nature of his illness. Attempts to obtain environmental support decrease as others age and become less tolerant of the patient's demands. Those who are troubled are likely to be involved with others who are also troubled and who may not be capable of supporting the patient's increasing needs. They too may react negatively, increasing the patient's vulnerability to suicide.

Thus, the significance of any one factor depends on the changing characteristics of other factors. Rarely are there isolated moments of specific stress in the backgrounds of suicide attempts, but rather continuing self-cycling patterns of interaction that, at times, reach psychologically intolerable proportions.

RELATIONSHIP TO SIGNIFICANT OTHERS

Significant others often criticize the patient's behavior and symptomatology, their intolerance of "abnormal" behavior serving to justify their inclination to assume a punitive custodial role.

Relationships characterized by excessive concern of the significant other for a dependent patient make it difficult for the patient to free himself from the relationship. Continued dependence may be rationalized by the patient in terms of lack of money, the need for a baby-sitter, or insufficient resources to move away from home. At times, patients are imprisoned in relationships by jealous significant others who prevent the patient from having contact with others by blocking incoming phone calls. For such patients, suicide becomes an assertion of the ego, the one step the patient can control.

Here, patients are once again faced with working through independence-dependence conflicts that so often have hampered them in their own personal growth in the past and and ill-prepared them to deal with the stresses and strains of daily living. Mary noted that her main problem was learning how to get along with her parents in a more suitable manner, to accept them, recognizing that they were not going to change and she was not going to change and how important it was for both parents and daughter to try to accept each other. Women who have difficulties in these areas often have difficulties establishing relationships with men.

Young women can have problems in finding compatible roommates. Marsha experienced difficulty in establishing relationships with her roommates, whom she always found to be self-centered. At work, she had difficulty relating to supervisors and managers. She acted in an overfriendly, unbusinesslike way with the supervisor, and noted: "When I am in close proximity to a man, I regard him as someone of the opposite sex, not as my boss or manager."

Personality problems are sometimes magnified by economic pressures, failure to maintain a job, unemployment, the experience of welfare, and the like. Separation from parents or chronic conflict with them creates a mixture of turbulence, isolation and lack of support for some patients.

Cities provide few opportunities in which anxious or inexperienced people can meet others and establish satisfactory friendships. Patients who return to the same chronic conflicts or sadomasochistic relationships or those attempting to establish new grounds have a relative paucity of opportunities to explore new ways of being or lack the confidence to try when opportunities present.

Suicide attempts often occur in association with difficulties in adjusting to shifts in relationships and residences. Young people in transition may encounter difficulties from failure to adapt to a life of their own without parental opposition, which may have provided them with a standard against which to judge their own conduct. The increase in freedom and the relatively unstructured nature of life in the city causes much anxiety for many who experience considerable uncertainty because of the variety of available activities and situations from which they are excluded or which makes choosing more difficult.

Young women are often exposed to a variety of unsatisfactory heterosexual contacts. As one young woman noted: "Lots of things about myself worry me. Such as my constant need to be reassured that I am loved by my closest friends, by Joe (in the things he does), even by my parents. Even when I know that someone cares about me or loves me, if they should do any little thing to make me doubt them in the least, I feel lost and alone again. I can't seem to help this even though many times I know for a fact that this feeling of mine is uncalled for. Also for some reason, there are many things I am afraid to do and I have to force myself (something as simple as going to the grocery store) for fear I'll make some sort of mistake. And I then feel very embarrassed and inferior. I feel as if everyone is looking at me, although I know they're not. I always feel much better if I have company in doing anything in which I come in contact with other people."

Stress on younger people derives from loneliness, shyness, debt, too much personal responsibility, and lack of parental support.

Many of the factors conducive to maladaptation result from the relative absence of community life in the city. For some, there are the singles' bars, where insincerity and role-playing characterize relationships. For others, there are courses to take, but rarely any continuity between school and social life. Life is fragmented and unless they become involved in a group, they find themselves remarkably isolated from existing social activity.

The city affords anonymity and freedom from small-town gossip and pressure to conform. Goal-directed individuals readily tolerate this. For psychologically dependent people, the anonymity of the city, the absence of meaningful relationships, the absence of continuity between activities and relationships and a relatedness to the remainder of the individual's life can be very stressful.

The pressures on married people in their thirties or forties present a different picture characterized by isolation, economic pressure, and a minimum of shared activity. When husbands work late, wives often feel isolated, lonely, and cut off. Money problems, the absence of mutual or shared goals, and the numerous realistic problems of rent, schools, and recreational activities create problems for the more vulnerable.

The stresses on the elderly, separated from their children who have moved to the suburbs, include the hardships of physical illness, isolation, crime in the streets, and lack of meaningful activity.

Environmental and economic factors contribute to the distress of elderly patients who have much less leeway to choose areas of residence. As one sixty-five-year-old woman noted, "My present neighborhood is dangerous. Even in the daytime, I'm afraid to go out." Wary of the people in the neighborhood, she remained there because of its familiarity and its proximity to her husband's job.

How commonly is isolation the setting for suicide? Social worlds may range from almost total isolation, as in the patient who has only peripheral contacts with delivery men, newsstands, or hotel clerks, to those who have superficial contacts at work, to those who are involved in meaningful relationships, to those who are overinvolved in particular relationships to the detriment of their personal freedom. The individual's contacts may be confined to family life or may involve more elaborate participation in community, religious, educational, social welfare, public welfare, and political organizations.

The social worlds of some patients may be restricted to their immediate families. Some may have peripheral contact with people encountered in the course of daily routines, such as restaurant personnel or neighbors, without major supportive relationships as a result of shyness or suspiciousness. The absence of meaningful social ties may prove socially disabling because these individuals lack the psychological support of others. This holds true more often for young men than for young women, who more readily enter into home situations.

The social world of some patients is further limited by the lack of contacts and satisfaction derived from personal relationships on the job, at home, or in the community. The lack of these sources of ego gratification and emotional support contributes to a lack of social development.

Hospitalization sometimes produces a rupture of existing relationships and makes it difficult for people to reestablish contact with others, particularly if their confidence has been undermined by the experience.

Occasionally, one encounters chronic patients in custodial-type environments. Such settings infantilize the patient, who is without responsibilities or privileges.

Minimal social expectations foster negative expectations that lead to incompetency and an inadequate self-image. Infantile behavior, the inability to take responsibilities, and poor personal hygiene may even result in such settings.

Patients such as this often remain helpless, even when asymptomatic. Exempting them from responsibilities, others often fear they might erupt with minimal provocation. In homes riddled by conflict, one often finds families resentful of the patient as a burden, yet unwilling to relinquish control or excessive in their demands that the patient enter the competitive world. Resisting suggestions to allow the patient to live alone, they may bolster their view by focusing on difficulties long since past.

What accounts for efforts to control the patient? Fear of recurrence most often leads to efforts to keep the patient in the chronic sick role and prevents patients from developing confidence in themselves and comfort in interpersonal relationships. The more the patient's views are challenged, the less certain he will be of his own perceptions. Ambivalent attitudes about the patient's competence to perform even the simplest of tasks, despite even prideful statements about the patient's "unusual gift and talents," make it difficult for the patient to distinguish fantasy from reality. Parental ambivalence encourages overliterate interpretation of nonverbal cues and reinforces dependency patterns. Where others deny their nonverbal communication, the patient's suspicions are heightened.

Overliterateness may lead to inflexibility and inability to adapt to the shifting expectations of others. Some patients try unsuccessfully to control their most minute actions. They may even think about which foot to put forward first, which hand to hold their fork with, and other simple acts that slow them up and cause them to miss the larger aspects of interpersonal situations.

Repeated errors evoke protective or rejecting responses from others. Perceptual and cognitive abnormalities thus produce a loss of confidence and alter the patient's behavior. While the family's response may also result from perceptual and cognitive defects, they usually respond with anxiety to issues relating to the patient's welfare, particularly in areas where the patient is least capable. Some, for example, praise the patient's brilliance, talent, and potential, reinforcing the patient's grandiosity, while burdening him with unrealistic expectations that generate anxiety and intensity.

Some families genuinely believe the patient cannot be trusted, even in simple areas of activity and responsibility, and they prohibit the patient from choosing his friends, using the family car, staying out late at night, handling money, or finding a job for himself.

Discouragement, direct prohibitions, or even threats of retaliation if the patient acts are rationalized as "being in the patient's best interests." Some families induce guilt by accentuating their self-sacrifices for the patient.

The family may seek to control the patient's activities by intruding into his or her relationships. Some families respond to slight shifts or difficulties in the patient's job situation, often intervening against the patient's wishes. The same interference may be manifested in schools, clinics, and hospitals, where the family may effectively undermine the patient's autonomy. They may then seek reassurance from the patient that they are still accepted.

The contradictions between the family's high expectations of the patient and strong limit setting, and between authoritarianism and a need for reassurance, confuse many patients. Several behavioral patterns may emerge from such contradictory expectations. Some patients ambivalently shift from guilt over not having done a task to guilt for having done it. Frustrated by parental inconsistency, they cannot express their anger against parents who have acted with "good intentions."

Rosalind W. lived in such a psychologically damaging home environment, where her angry and rejecting mother demanded extreme dependency. By presenting all problems to a "family council," she avoided responsibility and decision-making while maintaining a facade of being "democratic."

A vagueness about their identity and ego boundaries made it difficult for the patient to differentiate her own feelings from those of others. This resulted, at times, in marked selflessness and willingness to help others despite great personal expense and marked suffering. The more the patient gave to her mother, the more her mother expected. Therapy sought to strengthen the patient's confidence and ability to function without her mother's approval so that she would be able to act in terms of her own expectations rather than trying to fulfill her mother's unrealistic demands.

Failure to meet the expectations of others produces anxiety in patients with a blurred and uncertain sense of self. The distress results from feelings of inadequacy and from mixed feelings of hostility, guilt, and a failure to meet their own needs and pursue their own interests.

Some patients cannot differentiate between the quality of their performance and their unrealistic expectations of themselves, nor can they recognize that they need not live up to the "demands" of others. Inability to tolerate the negative reaction of others to their efforts to assume more responsibility for themselves, motivates a passive-dependency that in turn stifles their ability to assert themselves.

The dependency is in fact mutually binding and patients have difficulty in ignoring the expectations of others because of their reluctance to assume responsibility for themselves. Conversely, such patients fearful of rejection are often reluctant to relinquish responsibility for others.

Some patients, believing they cannot perform, rely on others who invariably prove incapable of acting, delay decisions, and finally find some excuse for inaction.

Unrealistic expectations and changing rules or requirements of behavior carry the implicit message that the patient has no rights because of his or her failure to function. Symptoms of illness justify a negative labeling of the patient. Ignoring the age and sex norms governing the behavior of the patient's peers, the family expects the patient to participate in social activities designed for other people, exposure to which often generates considerable anxiety for the patient that in turn is attributed to the patient's illness.

A twenty-five-year-old man may be expected to attend the "Sweet Sixteen" party of his sister's friend; an unmarried thirty-year-old woman may be expected to spend a dull afternoon with a group of married women and their babies.

Patients may be expected to return home at the same hour each evening, to review their social activities and to accept their family's judgments on their romantic attachments. Once married, some patients may be expected to continue to confide in parents and to allow them to comment, examine, and advise them about their marital relationship.

These expectations or "family traditions" effectively give the family control over the patient without any clear-cut recognition that such constraints may influence the patient's attitudes, expectations, and experiences. Patients may be expected to assume responsibilities for relatives, even when there is no justifiable reason or need to do so. Patients may be pressed into chauffeuring parents to the doctor and shopping centers. Typically, the request is made and the decision left entirely to the patient, who acts in terms of the implicit message rather than the literal request that would ordinarily allow him an out. To the extent that the patient gets angry because of the request, he feels even more obligated and guilty over his anger and even more motivated to be helpful in order to mask his anger.

The same applies in situations where a patient is asked to do a small favor for a relative, even if the favor is distasteful to him or if he will be put out by his efforts. Letting a sister use an apartment for a rendezvous or leaving an untrained dog in an apartment for a weekend or dropping in unexpectedly with unpleasant friends are examples of the subtle exploitation of patients through impositions in mundane areas. Where the patient experiences conflict and distress from these expectations, he may turn to the very same relative for support and relief of his "symptoms," which increases the patient's indebtedness to the relative.

Often, the relationship between patients and their parents or significant others is an attempt to mask the resentment and inhibited hostility generated by the fulfillment of these obligations. Patients do not resist such requests because of their fear of retaliation or fear of "hurting" others. Avoiding direct reference to distressing matters, they may communicate through intermediaries, another parent, an unrelated spouse, a doctor, or some willing go-between.

A relative may "confidentially" inform the third party about things the patient may be likely to say or do. Simultaneously, they may "confidentially" tell the patient that the third party knows something, thereby generating fears of conspiracy or confrontation. Belief in a conspiracy develops when the third party invites the patient to do something that the patient later on discovers has been prompted by the parent or spouse. This discovery sometimes leads to a blowup.

There is implicit in such transactions a notion of the patient's fragility and inability to know the facts about relationships and other things. Indeed, the very fact that a person raises any question about conspiracies may be taken as evidence that he requires special care. Occasionally, interference in a marriage by anxious parents jeopardizes the marriage. Conflicts may develop in patients who attempt to shoulder the burden of incompatible attitudes between parent and spouse.

Sometimes, others impose their values on a patient or insist on doing certain things in the patient's "best interest" that he cannot resist, since the implicit message is not to deny the significant other the opportunity to be helpful. Economic dependency may reinforce this pattern.

Significant conflicts develop from this intrusion into the patient's privacy, making it difficult for a patient to distinguish between fantasy and reality. To relieve their own anxieties, significant others press the patient to reveal intimate thoughts and feelings. Patients may even be asked for detailed reviews of dietary, sleep, bowel, and social habits. This information may later serve as the focus of criticism.

Where involuntary or physiological functions are focused on, the patient's vulnerability to criticism is increased. Sensitive to the attitudes of others, patients seek to avoid criticism by refraining from activities until significant others check out their plans and give them permission to proceed. In extreme cases, this has resulted in indecision and paralysis of action or the delusional belief that their thoughts were read and their feelings and actions controlled.

Overprotective relatives employ several tactics to keep patients in line. Patients have no reciprocal sanctions save symptom development or withdrawal. Conversely, there is an expected set of ways to behave that patients follow to be considered to be "cooperating," or "adhering to the rules of the game." The relatives' obligations are not specified, giving them greater freedom of action and enabling them to behave in contradictory ways without justifying themselves.

Relatives may rationalize their inconsistency by holding out the expectation of future rewards for cooperation, their own omnipotent fantasies being gratified by the patient's faith in their good intentions and promises.

The "rules of the game" change constantly, but always in such a manner that the relatives maintain dominance in the relationship. Arbitrary shifts in attitude are explained as necessary responses to the patient's behavior or symptoms and as justification for invading the patient's private space. Unable to challenge the significant others, patients often exaggerate their reliance on family. At times, a family ideology or mythology emerges, based on the notion that the patient cannot manage alone but must accept the infallibility and authority of the significant other in all areas of life.

This ideology and the ambiguous rules of the relationship enable parents to change the rules willy-nilly to maintain control. Ambiguity about parental desires and fear of censure keep the patient from reality, reinforce a negative self-image, and prevent him from gaining the support of others.

Relatives frequently try to impress people with their good intentions. Where, for example, the therapist allies himself with the patient, the parents, who have had a longer influence over the patient, invariably bring other sanctions to bear against the patient, including withdrawal of their support.

Some patients maintain numerous peripheral contacts with peer groups. These relationships range from fleeting contacts to emotionally taxing, mutually dependent relationships that undermine confidence and prevent the development of new ways of relating. Such relationships involve the relinquishment of autonomy and self-interest, obligatory responsibility for others, and loss of privacy. Such relationships occur with varying intensity in alcoholic, homosexual, and adolescent drug-taking groups, ostensibly formed around the particular activity. Critical observers of such groups, who condemn them for their self-indulgence or immoral behavior, generally miss their relative absence of choice or freedom to act. If anything, these relationships are noxious not so much because of the activity but because of the limits they impose on individual freedom.

When patients are involved with family or work relationships, they are better able to cope with these dominating peer groups. Where they have difficulties at home or on the job or lack other resources or interests, they are more likely to become increasingly absorbed in dominating peer groups.

The more the group membership is comprised of such people, the more demanding and dominating it tends to be. One should note the quasi-therapeutic self-help and relief seeking implicit in these groups through the use of pharmacologically active substances, the focus on personal matters, and peer support. In a sense, they resemble the more formal self-help groups that also provide support and reinforcement of neurotic needs, but are so structured as to reduce the chance of the individual becoming overinvolved in the pathological aspects of the group.

The same control over individual autonomy occurs in intense pathological relationships between two people. Disturbed individuals frequently involve themselves with other disturbed individuals in an effort at mutual support, which often backfires.

Chapter VIII

The Social Impact of a Suicide Attempt

THE suicidal act has social force and evokes responses in friends and relatives that affect the patient's subsequent clinical course. Most people generally deny any intention of attempting suicide. Some who believe they have overcome a preexisting inhibition may state that a repeated attempt in the face of stress or unremitting distress now seems feasible. The risk of a repeated attempt relates to the patient's mental status following the attempt. Those who continue to express futility, hopelessness, and suicidal thoughts are at greater risk than patients who have impulsively responded to acute transient stresses and have passed the crisis following the attempt.

Guilt over an attempt increases vulnerability in those who cannot limit the demands of others. Resentment and hostility develop from this, creating guilt and a return to the original crisis situation. A patient's efforts to act independently sometimes lead to increased oppression by friends, and efforts on their part to control the patient.

Some patients create hysterical crises by threatening suicide, involving many people in their experience. Knowing only part of the story, friends often act at cross purposes to each other, adding more turbulence to the situation. These patients may feel victimized and fail to realize their own role in the crisis. The anxiety and undisciplined response of others reinforce the patient's passive dependency and manipulativeness.

Some patients discover the secondary gains of being judged ill and continue to behave as if incapacitated. Some feel obligated to remain dependent so as to allow others the chance to help them. Relatives and friends often compete with the physician or therapeutic team, challenging the value of medication or criticizing the patient's efforts to improve. This creates confusion and obstructs the development of feasible objectives and goals.

Some patients isolate themselves from social groups and social activity, which reinforces their lack of direction and the intensity of stressful events. The elderly often lack goals and a purposeful role in the community. School dropouts similarly lack a sense of purpose and become involved in the drug subculture. This usually leads to increasing dependence on others.

Some patients return to noxious situations complicated by excessive involvement with relatives, children, and neighbors, by little privacy, and by continual frustration and guilt because of failure to meet the expectations of others. Some focus on the past, recriminating others or seeking revenge. Others focus on the future, experience anxiety and fear and avoid meaningful activity.

The suicide attempt often produces a change in attitude toward self, especially in cases where hospitalization or the initiation of treatment dramatizes the significance of the underlying disturbance. Treatment establishes the individual's right to be treated as a patient suffering from a treatable illness or condition as opposed to being treated moralistically as if he or she were a deviant. Failure to enter the role of patient may, however, reinforce the notion that the attempt is evidence of foolishness, lack of will power, or manipulativeness.

The social impact of attempted suicide can be broadly measured in terms of morbidity, divorce, separation, unemployment, and other manifestations of conflict and shifts in interpersonal or family relationships. Indeed, the risk of a repeated attempt remains high unless a realignment of relationships occurs or social conflicts subside.

The motives, conscious and unconscious, which govern suicidal behavior change during the course of a suicidal act. The motives operating at the moment of the attempt are often less significant than the irrational and uncontrollable tension state. Subsequent to the act, a concern for safety, feelings of regret, a desire for help, or other motives predominate.

Good environments can support the most psychiatrically disturbed patients. Noxious environments by contrast can be harmful to patients with less serious psychological disturbances and may even provoke repeated attempts. Environmental factors are most amenable to therapeutic intervention immediately following an attempt before the crisis has passed and the emotional responses of others have returned to the preattempt level.

Many tolerate custodial or brutal treatment from others who seek to control the patient for the patient's own "good." One man thrived on his wife's anxiety and dependency, and repeatedly criticized her while asserting that he was supporting her for fear that she could not function without his support and might attempt suicide.

Subtle rejection may manifest itself in the unwillingness of an already married suitor to commit himself to mar-

riage after an extended courtship. Such men may genuinely
promise to leave their wives, but cannot muster the confidence to relinquish their dependency on their wives. Individuals involved in such tenuous relationships often con-
vince themselves of their own inadequacy as an explanation
of the rejection. The relationship is jeopardized by their
own demands for more permanency.

A suicide attempt does not always modify relationships. If it is viewed as evidence that the patient has caused
the conflict, pressure on the patient may be intensified. The
absence of a supportive response to their attempts has led
some patients to withdraw from unsatisfactory relationships. Prognosis is guarded when a patient persists with a
fantasied hope of improved relationships. The husband of
one patient refused to visit her after her suicide attempt, although he continued to support her for various economic
reasons and was not willing to divorce her and even discouraged her from pursuing a divorce. She resigned herself to this fate and became increasingly occupied with
suicide.

The excessive dependency that emerges in such situations cannot readily be modified. Patients stubbornly resist
change and the necessary risks to develop healthy relationships. They may experience a multiplicity of negative emotions, chronic illness, personality problems, and unrealistic
attitudes that foster interpersonal conflict. Immature attitudes may conflict with authority. Perfectionistic attitudes
impede action and accomplishment. Suspiciousness fosters
isolation.

The attitudes of others contribute to the patient's self-
concept, emotional state, cognitive focus, and orientation
to action, which in turn reinforce the expectations of others.
Friends and relatives maintain their own stability by reinforcing attitudes most congruent with their own expectations. For this reason, the individual must consciously seek
to modify his self-concept by modifying his lifestyle and his

attitudes through psychotherapy and positive personal experiences.

Suicide attempts rarely lead to marked changes in self-concept. Few patients remain preoccupied or concerned with the attempt, acting almost as if it never occurred. Some, however, develop obsessive fears about feelings of inadequacy, hostility, envy, losing control, and acting out their "suicidal potential," attitudes reinforced by critical relatives and competitive school or job situations.

Such fears are frequently found in patients with heavy responsibilities, little privacy, and numerous distractions, which impede goal achievement. On the other hand, isolated living situations foster intensified feelings of loneliness, inadequacy, and alienation.

The stressfulness of any given environment depends on the patient's mastery of stress and adaptive skills and on the nature and quantity of existing stresses. A negative self-concept conditioned by the attitudes of others, an inclination to focus on the past or the future, and failure to focus on a meaningful objective intensify the sense of stress. Patients demoralized by their suicidal behavior may establish relationships with people who are insufficiently stable to provide supportive relationships.

RAMIFICATION OF TREATMENT—
INTERPERSONAL RELATIONSHIPS

Difficult interpersonal relationships with significant friends and relatives prove stressful for many. Sympathetic at first, relatives and friends often become unsympathetic, rejecting, and negativistic when their efforts to obtain favorable responses from the patient fail.

Improvement subsequent to the attempt depends very much on the treatment designed to help patients understand the nature of their underlying problems.

Many patients who attempt suicide in the wake of objectively stressful events improve after the stresses subside. Prognosis remains guarded, however, when the stress persists, as may be the case with physical disablement, continued unemployment, or other pressures.

Behavior patterns in need of modification often account for a patient's reluctance to enter treatment. Conversely, willingness to enter treatment and at times even the response to treatment can be viewed as facets of a patient's personality that influence the long-term prognosis. Sometimes, increased strength and self-interest foster increased conflict.

Interpersonal conflict causes problems for dependent patients threatened by the possible loss of a relationship. While conflict diminishes immediately after an attempt, it usually returns to its original level. If patients can understand the sadomasochistic exploitative patterns in their relationships, differentiate between their own objectives and the expectations of others, and reduce their inordinate sense of obligation to others, interpersonal conflict will subside. The adoption of life strategies conducive to greater self-realization reduces dependency and the interpersonal conflict that often results from it.

Therapeutic support can assist patients to cope with the reactions of others to the changes they undergo. Personality changes subsequent to an attempt may lead to shifts in relationships that create new pressures and new crises. Relatives and friends, willing to allow others to care for the patient, often reduce their efforts to assist the patient, which for some can be helpful and for others a form of rejection.

Failure to modify a negative life situation or strengthen the capacity to cope leaves unchanged the risk of repeated suicide attempts, depending on the persistence of factors precipitating the previous attempt.

Can a person withdraw from a sadomasochistic relationship? Definitely, if he receives reassurance in therapy and learns to distance himself from such relationships in order to obtain some objectivity.

By influencing whether or not patients enter into treatment and/or encounter, acute social factors significantly influence prognosis. Depressed patients generally experience more objective stress in their lives but enjoy better relationships than patients suffering from psychotic disorders or personality disorders. Repeated interpersonal conflicts characterize the experience of certain personality types.

Depressed patients with stable relationships have difficulty tolerating such conflicts and are more stressed by shifts in their relationships with others. Interpersonal conflict occurs more often among younger patients than among older ones. The older age groups generally have more stable relationships and less conflict, but more often experience the death of loved ones, physical illnesses, physical handicaps, and employment problems.

Some patients marry or divorce, others leave home. When patients make major changes in their lives precipitously thinking to resolve their problems, difficulties may persist. New living situations may tax a person's adaptive resources, especially if others minimize the validity of his distress and apply excessive pressure.

As the patient's capacity to change and handle stress improves, the prognosis improves.

Chapter IX

Outcome

$\mathbf{C}$AN subsequent suicide ever be predicted? Obviously, many of the factors considered thus far increase the risk of suicide but may not in themselves predict suicide. Someone may be depressed and preoccupied with suicidal thoughts and yet not attempt suicide, while someone else, following a relatively minor attempt, may do so.

Looking at the characteristics of the patients in our own investigation in relationship to various outcomes, one can see how complex the picture can be and how various combinations of factors interact to predispose the individual toward suicide. In our research, we obtained detailed information on 299 out of 300 patients one year or more after a suicide attempt to determine specifically what factors related to clinical outcome. The status of these patients was as follows:

Number	Percent	
25	8.3	much improved
104	34.7	improved
58	19.3	better
86	28.7	same
14	4.7	worse
7	2.3	dead from suicide
5	1.7	dead from natural causes
1	0.3	unlocated

It is illuminating to look at the general characteristics of the patients in these different groups.

DEAD FROM SUICIDE

The seven patients who died within a year from a repeated suicide attempt were predominantly former patients for whom the fatal attempt was their third attempt, yet there was nothing distinctive about their prior attempts, their psychiatric status, or their life experiences to suggest the likelihood that they would kill themselves. Some had made manipulative gestures in relation to pressing conflicts, some were psychotic, and some had suffered depressive reactions as a result of major reversals.

While they did not report significant interpersonal conflict, they regularly experienced a sense of rejection in relationships and had not experienced any significant changes in their lives during the year of follow-up. Indeed, most of them were considered to be difficult to reach in treatment by virtue of a general inability to suspend critical judgment and have faith in the treatment.

WORSE

Patients with unfavorable outcomes generally suffered from long-standing personality difficulties and had received much psychiatric treatment in the past, and reported an absence of major changes in their lives in the year subsequent to the attempt. They had histories of repeated suicide attempts; 50 percent had made moderate to severe attempts at the time of inclusion in our study. In the follow-up year, 70 percent made an additional attempt and 50 percent continued to report persistent suicidal thoughts.

While they often suffered from mild to moderate psychiatric illness, they developed difficulties because of chronic personality problems secondary to masochistic and dependent tendencies, and continued to be suicidal risks because of persisting stressful circumstances and interpersonal conflicts. Often, the attempt led to a change of attitude on the part of friends and relatives who adopted protective attitudes; the risk of suicide was often openly discussed and considered justification for excessive involvement in the patient's life, which often produced resentment and a perpetuation of the self-destructive cycle.

Patients who had not modified their life situations at follow-up were judged to be suicidal. Despite initially favorable responses to treatment, these patients soon reverted to alcohol or drug abuse and reestablished pathological relationships. The majority could not cope with added responsibilities of new jobs or marriage, and often made repeated suicide attempts under circumstances similar to the previous attempt.

Some unimproved patients experienced increased difficulties and a disruption of relationships. Others labeled as "dangerous" and "suicidal" entered custodial situations which undermined their confidence, reducing their chances for growth and maturation. Here, patients suffered abuse, ridicule, and criticism that fostered self-destructiveness prior to entry into treatment. Some neurotic, immature, or hysterical patients, unwilling to accept treatment, made repeated suicide attempts in a setting of continued conflict and rejection.

Repeated attempts often result from interpersonal conflict, frustration, alienation, and a sense of worthlessness. Patients who depended too much on others developed little self-confidence or self-reliance and unwittingly created additional pressures for themselves by seeking to meet the

conflicting expectations of others. The suicide attempt rep-
resented a form of self-assertion for them, a liberation from
inhibiting customs and dependent ties.

BETTER

Dramatic changes occurred in the lives of some patients after the suicide attempt. Almost half, however, continued to have the same conflicts as before. Thus, many
returned to unhappy marriages, sadomasochistic relationships or nonsupportive environments.

Patients in treatment, even those who experienced no
symptomatic improvement, gained insight into their problems, learning to identify the recurrence of symptoms, the
value of self-help, and the wisdom of avoiding turbulent situations. Most of all, they became less dependent on others.

Some patients moved into new and more satisfactory
situations. A close call with dying increased their apprecia-
tion of life, the attempt serving as a critical turning point
and treatment as an opportunity to refocus their resources.
Even when problems persisted, these patients progressed
because of changed attitudes and perspectives.

After experiencing initial difficulties in adjustment,
they created more circumscribed lives for themselves. This
reduced their vulnerability to stress and stabilized their expectations of others and of themselves.

Unlike patients who were unchanged or worse, these
patients proved flexible and willing to accept help. A reduction of dominating helpless tendencies reduced the sense
of frustration, the despair, and the hopelessness.

IMPROVED

Patients were rated as better when they had not made
a subsequent suicide attempt and had returned to premorbid functioning. Those who still had symptoms were respon-
sive to medication and supportive therapy. They cooperated with treatment and sought help whenever symptoms

or problems recurred. They also demonstrated the ability to pursue a goal-directed course.

While not highly disturbed, they had, in many instances, made quite serious suicide attempts. While the majority of these patients were functioning at work, in school, or at home at the time of the attempt, there were a number of seriously disturbed patients, several of whom were judged to be psychotic on admission but who showed remarkable improvement in the course of the year. Improvement for them resulted most often from a drastic shift in their lifestyle.

One young artist, recovered from a psychotic episode, moved to a rural area to avoid difficulty with people. In New York, she continually felt rejected, isolated, and pressured, and had no sense of her own identity. In the country, she purchased a horse and opened a riding school. Away from the turbulence of the city, she focused on riding lessons and painting, and renewed her long-lost confidence.

Other patients also focused on limited, well-defined goals, and adopted more realistic expectations about their abilities and a reduced sense of urgency about the necessity of immediate success. Thus, successful adaptation for the most disturbed patients resulted from disengaging themselves from overinvolved families and developing self-protective styles of living.

In effect, two-thirds of the patients who improved experienced changes in major areas of their lives in the year following their attempt. Only seven experienced no major changes; ten—change in work; five—change in residence (moved out of difficult situation); and two—change in marital status. These changes created a new stability and fortification against additional stress.

Much Improved

Much improved patients were those who functioned better in major life areas than they had in the year prior to the attempt. By definition, they were symptom-free and had no recurrences or repeated attempts in the year of follow-up. For the twenty-four patients much improved, the suicide attempt served as a stimulus to reevaluate themselves and to reorganize their lives. By and large, irrespective of diagnosis, the patients cooperated and responded to treatment and did not seek to establish dependent relationships.

Almost as many had made attempts serious enough to produce coma (or evidenced strong intent to injure themselves) as had made less serious or minimal attempts, suggesting that even patients who make dangerous suicidal attempts can have a good prognosis. All but seven had attempted suicide in a highly impulsive way. The methods they selected included fifteen overdoses, five lacerations, and four jumps.

While few of the patients who were much improved gave lifelong histories of psychiatric illness or major interpersonal difficulties, all had made previous attempts. Of the twenty-four patients, two had made one previous attempt; fourteen—two; six—three; and, two—four. While most patients with good outcomes had made minimal attempts, a number of patients were judged to have moderate to severe ratings on overall lethality and were given guarded prognoses at the time of entry into the study. Ten of the twenty-four patients with good outcomes continued in treatment through the end of the year, while fourteen discontinued treatment before the end of the year.

The birth of a child brought a new meaning to the life of one patient and helped her reconcile her marital conflicts. A new job, removed from the conflicts of an office romance, reduced the pressure on another young woman. A new home away from critical foster parents helped one patient with cerebral palsy.

Symptomatic improvement generally occurred concurrently with improved life circumstances. A shift to less stressful work or to a more satisfying living situation, relative to the patient's own values, was the crucial thing. For some, the key was the resumption of old interests, such as painting or the start of a new career even at "a late stage in life."

Considerable improvement occurred in patients with severe psychiatric disorders when they could modify the underlying circumstances. Learning to recognize how they created difficulty for themselves facilitated these shifts out of frustrating, conflict-producing situations not compatible with their temperament or adaptive skills. The pursuit of activities relating to personal strengths and interests led to more meaningful and supportive relationships and a revitalization of drive and motivation. To do this often required active seeking of new experiences and risk-taking to maximize potential.

By contrast, those who were worse or who died after one year could not mobilize themselves to make significant changes in their life situation or lifestyle so as to maximize their strengths and assume responsibility for themselves. These patients showed progressive deterioration after a history of life difficulties and poor relationships that complicated their illnesses.

An opportunity to reduce involvement in ongoing relationships and to look objectively at life helped to improve prognosis. The patients who were worse or dead at the end of one year were unable to gain enough objective perspective to actively pursue positive goals when they left the hospital. Most often they returned to their old circumstances and were unable by virtue of psychopathology or circumstances to start functioning in a purposeful goal-directed way.

Can one pinpoint high-risk types and therefore predict with some reliability the likelihood of suicide? In an effort to answer this question, we analyzed the data and established seven profile types by means of cluster analysis (Kiev, 1976). The following descriptions characterized the seven profile-types.

TYPE I: SUICIDAL GESTURE

Type I, the largest clustering, consisted of patients with characterological problems who experience few symptoms of anxiety, guilt, or depression; minimal dysfunctioning; minimal interpersonal conflict; and little alcohol and/or drug abuse. Denying the presence of psychiatric difficulties or attributing their problems to situational factors, patients who fitted this profile type made the least severe attempts of all seven groups. They reported no plans for the attempt, minimal suicidal intent, no real desire to die, minimal suicidal thoughts, and minimal discomfort before the suicide attempt. They attempted suicide with pills or by slashing their wrists in the presence of others or with others nearby, although no significant others were available for interview at the time of admission. Despite repeated low-risk attempts, these patients tended to have good general outcomes; they showed little increase in conflict or in symptoms at one- and two-year follow-up.

TYPE II: ACUTE DEPRESSIVE REACTION

Type II, the second largest clustering, consisted of acutely depressed patients who believed themselves to be incapable of coping with objective life stresses and attempted suicide with irreversible means in a setting that held minimal possibilities of rescue.

These patients reported the highest scores on the somatic symptoms of depression, including appetite, sleep, and sex disturbance, as well as high scores on anxiety, tension, fear, and remorse. They reported minimal interpersonal conflict with significant others, who tended to be supportive.

The social setting of the suicide attempt of this group

of patients—at a distance from others and with minimal possibility of rescue—earmarked this high-risk group. In the year following the attempt, these patients showed the highest scores on increased conflict, the second highest scores on subsequent hospitalization, and relatively high scores on increased symptoms and some subsequent attempts.

Hospitalization should be seriously considered for this group of patients. They require prompt reduction of depressive symptoms with ECT or psychopharmaceuticals. Special precautions should be taken when a patient who fits this type appears to improve but has not yet come out of his depression.

TYPE III: PASSIVE-AGGRESSIVE AND PASSIVE-DEPENDENT PERSONALITY DISORDERS

Type III patients reported a minimum of symptoms and interpersonal conflict. Judged by significant others to be quite dysfunctional, these patients had been hospitalized in the past more often than any of the other groups. They attempted suicide in a remote and private way, using irreversible means and making no effort to obtain help. In the year following the attempt, they made the fewest major changes in their lives and were judged generally to have the worst clinical outcomes, despite the absence of repeated attempts. They scored none or minimal on ratings of suicidal preoccupation and obsessive thoughts or acts. They showed little evidence of emotional or physical blunting of affect and received the lowest scores on unusual thoughts and behavior of any of the groups. They also had mild and minimal ratings on grandiosity, hallucinatory behavior, and bizarre thought content. They were rated as minimal to mild on anxiety, guilt, tension, and depressive symptoms.

A history of a serious suicide attempt in an isolated social setting without the seeking of help and a discrepancy between these patients' views of their problems (they minimized them) and the views of significant others (who may have been indifferent, rejecting, punitive, or overcontrolling in their concern for the patients' welfare) made this a high-risk group.

Treatment goals for patients who fit this type must be designed to reduce their high rate of dropping treatment. Brief hospitalization should be considered to reduce the pressures brought by significant others and to arrange less noxious living arrangements for these patients. Long-range supportive programs may prove to be the most satisfactory way of keeping contact with them. At the same time, significant others should be helped to reduce their excessive guilt and sense of responsibility.

TYPE IV: ANXIETY REACTION WITH INTERPERSONAL CONFLICT

Of the seven groups, Type IV patients were judged to have the highest scores on tension, suicidal threats, and interpersonal conflict despite reports of significant others that they were supportive and nonthreatening. While patients who fit Type IV attempted suicide in close proximity to others with reversible methods—e.g., lacerations and pills—they were judged to be above average in suicidal potential.

Type IV patients received average scores for unusual thoughts and emotional and physical blunting, and the lowest scores for depressive symptoms and overall dysfunctioning. They seemed to be making good adjustments.

The most prominent feature of this group appeared to be the marked discrepancy between the patients' high scores for interpersonal conflict and the significant others' accounts of being supportive, which no doubt contributed to the persistence of high levels of interpersonal conflict, the highest incidence of repeated attempts, and the second highest scores on symptoms in the year following the attempt. These patients reported considerable interpersonal conflict with significant others, who viewed themselves as supportive and minimizing the patient's distress. The discrepancy between the patient's subjective sense of rejection and the reports of the significant others' indifference led to repeated attempts, a persistence of symptoms, and continued interpersonal conflict.

Treatment for this group of suicide attempts must ultimately focus on the resolution of interpersonal conflict and reduction of related anxiety and tension. Outpatient treatment and family therapy may be most relevant because hospitalization is unlikely to resolve the problem.

Type V: Socially Isolated

Type V patients, who are characterized by very high scores on interpersonal conflict, suicide potential, and unusual thoughts and behavior, attempted suicide at a distance from others and made no effort to be rescued. Despite this, significant others judged their functioning to be unremarkable, a finding with substantial prognostic implications. Of interest and possibly related to their social isolation, Type V patients (like Type VII patients, described below) could not be personally evaluated at the time of the one-year follow-up.

The inclination of this group of patients to drop out of treatment should be recognized. Efforts should be made to establish a long-range supportive and contact program for these patients, with simultaneous efforts directed toward the education of significant others, who must be helped to understand the seriousness of the problems of these patients.

Type VI: Suicidal Preoccupation

Type VI patients constituted a group who were diagnostically similar to Type I patients except for high scores on unusual thoughts and behavior and the highest score of any group on suicide potential. These patients reported more obsessive thoughts and interpersonal conflict than Type I patients, although their scores were close to the mean. They experienced little anxiety, guilt, or depressive symptoms and only minimal dysfunctioning. They were close to the mean on emotional withdrawal and physical blunting, and they attempted suicide in close proximity to others.

At one year, Type VI patients had made the most major changes. They had high scores on increased symptoms but had made no subsequent suicide attempts.

In essence, Type VI patients presented more serious characterological problems than Type I patients, as well as the highest scores on the factor measuring suicide potential. They made relatively nonserious attempts in close proximity to others in the face of situational problems but appeared to have good one-year outcomes, probably related to the major changes they were able to make in their lives.

TYPE VII: CHRONIC DYSFUNCTIONAL

Type VII patients resembled Type III patients in that they had low scores on anxiety and guilt and attempted suicide at a distance from help, using irreversible means. They also had high scores on interpersonal conflict, suicide potential, and significant others' ratings of overall dysfunctioning and rejection.

They differed from Type III patients in that they had higher scores on obsessive thoughts, suicidal preoccupation, and overall dysfunctioning, the highest scores on emotional and physical blunting, and some evidence of depressive symptoms.

It is, therefore, possible to group patients and establish clinically consistent profiles that cut across traditional diagnostic lines and that consider the complexity of simultaneously operating variables. These profiles hold up over time, and there is a demonstrated empirical consistency to them that gives them prognostic significance. The high correlation between initial and outcome variables supports the validity of the profiles, which have been theoretically and statistically determined.

Chapter X

Implications
for Treatment
and
Prevention

A TTEMPTED suicide cannot be lightly dismissed
as either "attention-seeking" or as "not serious."
People who attempt suicide often come close to death.
Others who make less serious attempts may kill themselves
subsequently.

Most patients express ambivalent feelings about death
and indirectly communicate their suicidal intentions well
in advance of acting. In this sense, suicide attempts do not
occur unpredictably and can be prevented if proper attention is paid to the distressed person.

The suicide crisis may be turned into an opportunity
to alert patients to important previously obscure but soluble
problems. It can prove to be a turning point, especially if
individuals seek professional help and a treatable condition
is discovered. The suicidal crisis provides the stimulus for
many to take a new and different look at themselves and
their relationships with others. Frequently, more healthy

and satisfying ways of living and relating evolve from the changes that occur during and after the crisis.

Interpersonal conflicts cause the most problems for dependent people unable to modify their relationships or who are threatened by the possible loss of a relationship. Immediately after an attempt, interpersonal conflicts diminish. Some relationships even improve for a brief time, but eventually return to their previous level. In cases where the patient can understand the exploitative patterns in his relationships, define his own objectives and the expectations of others, and reduce his sense of obligation to others, the interpersonal conflicts subside. The adoption of life strategies conducive to greater self-realization reduces dependency and the interpersonal conflict that often results from it.

Difficult interpersonal relationships with significant friends and relatives often prove to be the most stressful kinds of relationships. Sympathetic at first, relatives and friends often become unsympathetic, rejecting, and negativistic when their efforts fail to obtain favorable responses from the patient. Improvement subsequent to an attempt depends very much on those attitudes in friends and relatives and the patient as well, which helps some patients to understand their problems and better cope with them.

Therapeutic support is particularly valuable for patients encountering negative reactions from others resentful of their new strength and self-interested patterns. Lack of attitude change in treatment of life situations augurs a poor prognosis. The prognosis is better when an attempt has been precipitated by external, objective, modifiable factors unlikely to recur.

The social environment influences whether or not patients enter into treatment and/or encounter continued conflicts or stress. Repeated interpersonal conflict characterizes certain immature personality types as well as younger people. Other stresses, such as the death of a loved one, physical illness, physical handicaps, and employment problems, predominate in older patients. Changes in personality and in the role assumed subsequent to the attempt sometimes lead to shifts in the environment and new pressures, which often precipitate new crises. Friends and relatives, willing to allow others to take responsibility for the patient's welfare, often reduce their efforts. This can be helpful for some patients, but others, fearful of being stigmatized or of losing control, begin to regress.

Others marry, divorce, leave home, or make other major changes in their lives. Where such actions are viewed as solutions to unresolved problems, the patient is likely to persist in his or her difficulties. The requirements of new living situations often tax the patient's adaptive resources, especially where others deny the validity of the patient's illness and emphasize the need for greater will power.

At times, noxious environmental factors produce more stress. Retaliatory responses to stressful interpersonal relationships increase the risk of repeated attempts because of the cognitive inability of patients to control their impulses. Some individuals improve by virtue of maturation or therapy, and the prognosis changes.

√ The risk of a repeated attempt closely relates to the patient's understanding of his problems, his faith in the possibility of modifying his life situation, and the nature of his interpersonal relationships. Patients with histories of repeated attempts require special treatment programs designed to help them master their impulsivity. Careful control of drug- and alcohol-abuse patterns is especially important in impulsive repeaters. For some, guilt over the attempt heightens their sense of helplessness and increases their vulnerability to the views and demands of others. Resentment and hostility often develop from this, creating more guilt and repeated crises. Efforts to act independently sometimes lead significant others to intensify their control of the patient. These interactions require modification by appropriate psychotherapeutic intervention.

Patients should be encouraged to modify specific behavior patterns that generate negative reactions in others. Patients who feel victimized by others may find, for example, that their own dependency and manipulativeness induces controlling behavior in others.

The suicide attempt often produces a change in attitude toward self, especially where hospitalization or the initiation of treatment dramatizes the significance of an underlying disturbance. Treatment establishes legitimate entry into a sick role as opposed to a deviant role. This is not always without its attendant complications. Some patients discover the secondary gains of the sick role and continue to behave as if incapacitated. Some feel obligated to remain dependent, so as to allow friends and relatives the chance to feel helpful.

But, by and large, failure to accept the sick role reinforces incorrect notions of the attempt as evidence of foolishness, lack of will power, or manipulativeness. This also occurs when significant others challenge the value of treatment or criticize the patient's efforts to improve. This creates confusion and obstructs the development of feasible objectives and goals.

The risk of suicide increases when others make moral judgments about the patient, failing to recognize he is suffering from a treatable condition. Their expectations can produce a significant impact on the patient's behavior and may have to be modified to assist the patient. Many significant others fail to acknowledge the presence of a treatable illness or reaction pattern.

A wide range of beliefs and attitudes contribute to this nonrecognition of psychiatric disorder and emotional conflict. Relatives and friends often refuse to recommend treatment or adopt critical attitudes toward nonfunctioning or symptomatic patients. These attitudes complicate the patient's problems and sometimes precipitate suicidal crises. While familiar with concepts of mental illness and able to correctly identify descriptions of abnormal behavior, significant others often have difficulty in recognizing actual cases of mental illness and making recommendations for treatment. This is particularly so when it occurs in family members. Relatives minimize or deny the manifestations of mental illness and postpone recommendations of treatment. Ambiguous and fluctuating moods complicate the recognition of suicidal intent. Symptoms of anxiety and urgency increase the chances of recognition.

The tolerance of symptoms and the criteria for entry into the sick role vary from patient to patient. Many do not seek help. If they seek medical treatment, their psychiatric problems are sometimes missed. At times, patients enter treatment but stop when they fail to get prompt relief, encountering little opposition to this even when the need persists. Relatives sometimes support nonadherence to the physician's recommendations, and accept the patient's etiological formulations about social problems, which often become the focus of treatment to the neglect of treatable symptoms.

The early somatic symptoms of depression include: insomnia, compulsive eating, anorexia, loss of energy, palpitations, shortness of breath, decline in libido, and somatic aches and pains that may be attributed to external stresses or personality weaknesses.

The plausibility of these rationalizations makes the recognition of illness less likely in the face of the patient's denial of depression and the acceptance of his rationalizations by others. The resemblance of depressive symptoms to the common emotional reactions to everyday-life experiences makes it difficult to judge the severity of depression. Mildly and moderately disturbed patients whose symptoms go unrecognized are at greater risk of suicide than the more obvious cases of severe depression or schizophrenia, more likely to be referred to a hospital or to a psychiatrist.

Psychological vulnerability often changes more than

environmental factors, which are most subject to change
at the time immediately surrounding the attempt. A major
objective of treatment is the modification of stressful environments. Helping patients focus on goals and opportunities for satisfaction through achievement facilitates such
change. Lack of goals too often leads to an excess dependence on interpersonal relationships to provide a sense of
gratification, leading to excessive dependence on others,
fear of rejection, and personal compromise, which in turn
lead to intensification of guilt, anger, and resentment.

   When possible, therapy should seek to educate patients to anticipate problems, to learn to by-pass obstacles,
to learn alternative ways for dealing with stress, and to stop
relying on such maladaptive solutions as alcohol and drug
abuse. It is especially important for suicidal patients to
learn to maximize their sense of self-confidence and overcome doubts by setting realistic goals, and reducing exposure to the pressure from others.

   The suicidal act has social force and evokes a range
of responses in the patient and in friends and relatives that
affects the patient's subsequent course. The response to suicide attempts varies from patient to patient and from time
to time in the same patient. It is therefore important to involve significant others in the overall management of suicidal patients.

   Active intervention is especially necessary in situations
where significant others infantilize patients by focusing on
the attempt or the patient's inadequacies, subtly reinforcing
a negative identity. Such environments foster dependency
and uncertainty and prevent the individual from establishing
and reaching personal objectives. They often hold on to unrealistic fantasies that things will improve despite clear-cut
evidence to the contrary.

   When patients create problems for others by means
of their behavior, they are very likely to be identified either
as "crazy," and therefore in need of the chronic sick role,

or as "overreacting" and "neurotic" and not in need of treatment, as in the case of the depressed, or as the kinds of people who are hysterical personalities, like the alcoholics, who tend not to be treated with sympathy by others, but more in terms of controls. Such patients evoke attitudes in others that mitigate against their receipt of appropriate treatment. Negative or oversolicitous attitudes of significant others heighten the patient's sense of worthlessness and hopelessness.

Treatment programs must be specifically geared to the characteristics of the suicide syndrome. The high incidence of discomfort and impulsivity before the attempt point to the importance of a treatment approach and an attitude that places great emphasis on the maximization of the patient's capacity to tolerate anxiety and discomfort and to the development of strategies for daily living that enhance the patient's capacity to resist environmental pressures.

Essentially, this orientation calls for a rational preventive approach that emphasizes the prompt reduction of the patient's sense of guilt, the conscious acquisition of better habits, and the adoption of a positive orientation toward coping.

The assessment of the family and/or significant people in the patient's life is a crucial part of the evaluation of the suicidal potential of patients. The decision to return a patient to the same environment in which the attempt occurred must take into consideration the extent of concern of others, the lack of awareness of the seriousness of the illness, absence in the environment of marked conflict and undermining attitudes, a recognition of the need for therapy, and a willingness to delay major life changes until the patient has recovered.

The most important role of the family or significant others in the treatment of the patient is the support given to the patient's entry into the "sick role." This involves a recognition by the significant others and the patient that the patient is not responsible for his condition, is technically incompetent to handle or resolve the condition alone, and that much of his distress results from failure to enter the sick role.

These recommendations are in agreement with the conclusions of Moss and Hamilton, who emphasized that the family must be involved in the treatment (Moss and Hamilton, 1956). Farberow and McEvoy have similarly noted the importance of integrating the family with the treatment process. "Discharge to the family or to the same environment which fostered his disturbance, without any change having occurred in the environment, merely invites a recurrence of the disturbance and suicidal acting out" (Farberow and McEvoy, 1966).

The correlations between significant others' attitudes and prognosis emphasize the importance of consulting with the significant others at the time of first contact with potentially suicidal individuals.

Understanding the patient's long-term relationships with others may have more prognostic significance than the immediate responses of significant others that are colored by the urgencies of the moment following the suicide attempt. Our investigations underscore the value of inviting participation of the significant others in the therapeutic program, so as to influence their attitudes and behavior toward the patient before old attitudes reappear.

The attitudes of friends and relatives toward the patient's acceptance of the sick role relate to interpersonal conflict, hospitalization, and major changes, which have significance for patient management. Special attention must be paid to the discrepancies between attitudes about the relationship that may exist between patients and friends and relatives.

Even when friends and relatives have a genuine interest in the patient, the patient may view them as part of his or her problem. Distinguishing between support and control can prove useful. Supportive attitudes must be carefully defined in each instance, so that significant others do not assume responsibility for the patient, thereby limiting his opportunity to grow by handling his own problems. Significant others can be helped to remain interested without having to shift from being oversupportive and overprotective to outspoken martyrs, who induce guilt in the patient by expressing feelings of rejection for having had their help turned down.

The psychiatrist must carefully weigh the contribution of significant others to the patient's problems, which may not be apparent at the time of the attempt, when they are likely to be showing concern. Often, they control their anger with the patient and seek to hospitalize him or her in part for punitive reasons. Significant others may thrive on the patient's dependency or welcome the martyr role and want to hospitalize the patient because the suicide attempt has demonstrated an independence that threatens the relationship.

Social attitudes contribute to self-concept, emotional state, cognitive focus, and action orientation, all of which influence the individual's behavior and in turn the expectations of others about the individual. These attitudes can be changed only by active intervention. Different situations produce different effects on the individual's self-concept, emotional state, cognitive focus, and action orientation. For this reason, different groups of patients require a different emphasis in the treatment process. The individual living at home is subject to different pressures than the individual living in a custodial hospital or prison, where a suicide attempt may set in motion a process of negative labeling.

Ideally, the significant others ought to be included in the treatment process. When the patient is admitted to a hospital, provisions for modifying family attitudes and expectations should be made so that when the patient returns home, he or she will not be exposed to the same factors that may have precipitated hospitalization. Special attention must be paid those who refuse to enter into treatment programs. Such patients generally prove to be more susceptible to subsequent difficulties than those who are able and willing to recognize and identify depressive behavior disorders within themselves.

Patients who regain their composure rapidly and deny suicidal impulses following an attempt pose special problems. We have found that willingness to accept continued contact with the psychiatric facility after the initial phase of the suicidal crisis is an important criterion of the suicidal potential of the individual. Patients with the worst prognosis were those who were reluctant to accept treatment or cooperate with the follow-up.

Seventy-three percent of our patients were not in treatment three months prior to the attempt, although many had been troubled for considerable periods of time. Most did not feel that they were ill or that their symptoms required treatment. Most believed their symptoms would pass. Symptoms were usually rationalized in terms of life difficulties or the patient's personality. Only 21 percent attributed their difficulties to what they considered a psychiatric illness.

Only 4 percent of the patients in our sample called a suicide-prevention number prior to their attempt. The suicidal act in most was characterized by impulsivity and absence of premeditation, even in the most dangerous attempts.

Patients were often so emotionally disturbed at the time of the attempt that they not only did not consider, but could not use the telephone to call for help. It is likely that those who kill themselves are similarly disturbed and cannot call for help at the moment of maximum suicidal drive. Another factor, which cuts across sex, age, and the diagnostic groups, was nonrecognition of an underlying psychiatric illness or emotional disturbance that the patient was experiencing prior to the attempt.

It is also important to pay attention to the different patterns of suicidal behavior, which respond differently to conventional forms of psychiatric treatment. In our own experience, we have had considerable difficulty in preventing repeated attempts in certain impulsive patients, irrespective of the approach used, although in a number of instances treatment may have reduced the frequency of repetitive attempts and shortened the time required for psychological recovery from them. Many of these patients who made repeated attempts have been in touch with family physicians and/or psychiatrists and indeed in a fair percentage of cases, had received adequate antidepressant therapy and psychotherapy. These facts suggest that such efforts may do little for impulsive, immature patients who make repeated attempts.

Quite clearly, high-risk groups need special attention to help them contain their self-destructive impulses. This relates to the importance of having the authority to persuade people about their need for specific help when they are sick, for their own benefit and in terms of the effect on others. It is difficult to legislate control over psychiatric disorders even when these have ill effects on the lives of others. This is difficult to prove and is usually considered an invasion of privacy. Here such things as the battered-child syndrome, a range of noxious effects of maternal deprivation, the burden on others generated by neurosis and psychosis are the kinds of things one might consider to be in an area where social legislation might indeed be appropriate once more substantial evidence is in.

We need new techniques for reaching high-risk groups in ways that consider their special features—alcoholics, autocides, and so forth. Knowledge of early prehistory of such cases is important; e.g., underachievement or delinquency may be early warning signs. Glue sniffing may indicate greater likelihood of increased difficulty later on. Other early clues would include such factors as nonacceptance of treatment and sadomasochistic relationships.

Suicidal patients are difficult to treat. Repeated impulsive suicide attempts and frequent suicidal threats tax the therapist's patience. Such patients are prone to ambivalence, power struggles, and the like, which impede therapy.

Crisis-intervention techniques must be incorporated into traditional psychotherapeutic approaches, so that therapists can flexibly respond to the personality problems of these patients, which are manifested in reluctance to enter therapy, lateness, missed appointments, and disinclination to get involved in a therapeutic relationship. Those who do get involved in therapy are often very dependent and demanding and skilled at eliciting rejection or initiating crises.

To the extent that suicide attempts occur in predisposed individuals acting in response to the vicissitudes of life encountered by normal individuals, it may be possible to prevent them either by paying special attention to the normal population undergoing special vicissitudes or by focusing efforts on the people of greatest risk. Life-strategy classes for those about to encounter special stresses may be valuable as a preventive measure.

Life-strategy classes, first developed in the management of depressed and suicidal patients, are now being used to train relatively healthy individuals as well. The classes focus on cognitive restructuring reflexes rather than on emotional catharsis, and are conducted as seminars with a mental health worker as leader.

Highly dependent individuals, for example, tolerate bereavement much less well than independent and resourceful individuals. The elderly often need the assistance of social services, particularly when they have built their life around a spouse. Serious physical illness and fewer social roles in the older age groups reduce flexibility and adaptability. Chronic persistent stresses create more serious problems than discrete episodes of objective stress which do not last. Persisting noxious relationships are perhaps the most troublesome type of stress.

Maladaptive patterns include excessive confessions to others, efforts to make amends for past wrongdoings, failure to pursue self-interest, and involvement in complicated relationships. An increase in risk-taking behavior, alcohol abuse, and drug abuse often indicates a deflection of self-destructive trends into less obvious forms. Here strategies for behavior modification would include:

1. Capitalizing on past experiences.

2. Dealing with stress through the acquisition of information and focused activity.

3. Turning error, failure, and criticism into rewarding, satisfying, and profitable learning experiences.

4. Creating positive thought models; mastering "alarm" responses.

5. Understanding and overcoming the unconscious factors that motivate fear.

Reality factors, such as job pressures and housing shortages, add extra burdens. Step-by-step planning techniques prove useful here:

1. Establishing goals that focus on the present.

2. Planning the next day's activities.

3. How to keep from overcommitting one's self.

4. Establishing priorities.*

Study of the natural history of suicidal behavior suggests that early recognition of clues to suicide is possible. We now need to be able to differentiate normal patterns of behavior for a particular group from pathological patterns.

Drug abuse may, for example, be the norm in youth

---

*For more detail, see my paper: Psychotherapeutic Strategies in the Management of Depressed and Suicidal Patients, *Amer. J. Psychotherapy,* 29: 345-354, 1975.

subcultures and not necessarily indicate psychopathology. Greater sensitivity to different risk groups in different clinical settings is also needed. Those with serious psychiatric disorders, the manic-depressive psychoses, and the schizophrenics are high-risk groups in certain phases of their illness. The delinquent with a low frustration threshold is at greater risk in his twenties and thirties than later on when he has stabilized. This contrasts with obsessive-compulsive neurotics whose risk increases with age and with declining ability to maintain perfectionistic standards.

It would be extremely valuable to establish case registers and periodic examinations for such high-risk individuals on a larger scale at the community or municipal level. This ought to have considerable effect in reducing the high rate of repeated attempts and completed suicides among high-risk groups. Attention needs also to be given to measures limiting the availability of lethal agents, such as gun control, poison control, and closer surveillance of the distribution of barbiturates.

ADDITIONAL PREVENTIVE MEASURES

Vulnerable individuals outside of the treatment network must be exposed to new information, knowledge about the basic signs and symptoms of psychiatric disorder and emotional distress, knowledge of those resources in the community to which they can turn for obtaining assistance in handling problems as well as knowledge about how to negotiate the complexities of bureaucratic medical systems. These people, as well as those within medical networks, have considerable misinformation and beliefs in numerous myths about suicidal behavior and depressive psychiatric illness.

We must develop paraprofessionals to reach those outside the present treatment network. Ideally, members of the subculture have the most access to the population, and often can influence the acquisition of the knowledge necessary for suicide-prevention work. Existing agencies, such as medical schools, can serve as the base for such community-oriented programs.

The need for follow-up, the use of gatekeepers, and many nonpsychiatric helping institutions argues for a type of organization of manpower and resources that utilizes a minimal central facility (possibly a computer) and a large field team whose training and data-collecting procedures are standardized and who, making periodic contact with community agencies, can enlarge the picture of suicidal phenomena and increase the delivery of knowledge to peripheral facilities. In the past several years, we have met with representatives of over a hundred agencies, hospitals, and the like in Manhattan to discuss these issues and, in general, have found a widespread consensus on the need for such an operationalized liaison program. This has special relevance for facilities and physicians, drug-abuse programs, and the like.

We must identify and thereby reduce those kinds of noxious environmental factors that undoubtedly contribute to increasing suicidal risk in different subculture groups. What special stresses are created for various groups? What are the generic stresses of industrialization, urbanization, migration, and mobility? What differentiates suicidal and nonsuicidal individuals in these different groups?

Our study suggests that high scores on objective stress relate to seriousness of suicide attempts. This suggests that modification of stress may contribute to a reduction in suicidal behavior. Clearly, stresses vary in different subcultural groups and contribute to variations in vulnerability as age and environment change.

Younger suicide attempters give histories of nonperformance, noteworthy or antisocial behavior, and a general lack of involvement in the social system. As these patients grow older, they may be under less pressure to perform, utilizing social categories of disability, retirement, or unemployment as excuses for not performing. By contrast, striving, ambitious, and conscientious people who cope with life stresses may not adapt readily to retirement. Successful businessmen and professionals may encounter severe blows to their self-esteem from economic reverses or declining standards when they are older and cannot handle reverses as well.

Preventive programs should be tailored for specific groups. An executive needs more preparation for his retirement than does a blue-collar worker, whose leisure hours may always have received his primary attention. Retirement may provide him with more time to do what he has always been doing in his spare time.

The establishment of a link between life stresses and suicidal behavior will also have significance for treatment approaches. Treatment may be significant if it reduces the number of life changes in the individual's life and stabilizes it. If it increases the number of changes, even if these are deemed desirable, it will increase the risk of suicidal behavior. The implications for treatment and prevention from this model are clear: reduce change in the patient's life.

The suicide rate among men is considerably higher than among women, and yet the attendance of men in psychiatric clinics and in psychiatric office practice is considerably lower. In our society, men do not enter the sick role readily. Active links should be established with industry, school, prisons, and other institutions to increase awareness among leaders and problem-solvers of the early signs and symptoms of suicidal crisis.

There is an urgent need for the development of training programs in the early recognition of psychiatric disorders and the initial phases of crisis intervention for ministers, union counselors, management consultants, community mental health workers, and others, who in the course of their daily work come into contact with high suicidal risk individuals with treatable symptoms, which are masked by other complaints, explained away by reasonable explanations, or justified as understandable responses to stressful events. More specific knowledge of the natural history of specific suicidal patterns would facilitate such training programs.

Appendix 1

A Daily Checklist for Patients

1. Make an active effort to rely on yourself. Above all, minimize your doubts about yourself, your abilities, and the adequacy of your preparation for a particular task. More emphasis should be placed on the honesty, integrity, and emotional intensity with which you approach a particular task, for ultimately, it is the intensity of involvement that accounts for the results. If properly approached, your work can be rewarding and can enable you to minimize the distractions that reduce emotional stability and mental effectiveness. You must establish goals and pursue them, whatever the course.
2. Postponement can become habitual and can lead to nonproductivity. It may mean accommodation and revision of programs and schedules. You must recognize that when you postpone your involvement in something, you will probably never accomplish it. You will

be left in the future with memories of past wishes rather than of past deeds.

There is a great tendency to procrastinate, to focus on the future, or to be distracted by immediate desires and opportunities for self-indulgence. You must recognize that the present is crucial and that every day is another opportunity to gain strength and accomplish things. You need not be deterred by past experiences nor by the fantasy that the future will provide this opportunity. Unfortunately, if you wait, not only do you postpone the activity, but you may never realize your potential. All activity should be entered into with the notion that no matter how hard the task becomes, it is still most satisfying when you do it yourself.

3. You are likely to profit most if you seek satisfaction and joy in your work and also if you don't take it too seriously. To the extent that you enjoy what you do, you are likely to find it less like work and more like a satisfying game.

4. You should work to improve that which you do best and most readily, since this is your particular gift and one that should be maximized. You may run into opposition from others who will advise conformity. Don't permit them to influence you. There is nothing wrong with pursuing those things at which you are successful, even though what others recommend may on the surface appear to be more important. Others often suggest that a particular approach be pursued, and that unless you follow it, the work will not be acceptable or successful. Many people follow this kind of advice only to find that they have removed themselves from the very area of interest that led them to the work in the first place.

5. You must not succumb to the feeling that you have insufficient time to do what you want. Careful examination will show that you waste a lot of time with ex-

traneous activities and that a considerable amount of work can be accomplished in a short time if you devote yourself to it.

6. Approach the day in a relaxed way, letting things emerge and evolve as the day goes on. On the other hand, some minimal or general scheduling can be of value. Ultimately, however, you must deal with each minute as it comes instead of investing in the future before you have adequately dealt with the present. Above all, the work should be enjoyed as it is done. And, if for some reason you are out of work, move on to another activity. This is all relevant to mental health, since you can, by shifting from one activity to another as the spirit moves you, accomplish a great deal without becoming excessively involved in ruminations about any single activity.

7. Thus, the expenditure of time in relationship to activity becomes a crucial way for you to monitor your daily routines. If you try at all times to maximize the moment, you will be able to weigh the significance of any particular activity against the overall list of priorities you have. You can focus on the present in terms of these priorities so that you will minimize or halt those activities which have no real importance. In this way, you will be increasingly free of unnecessary pressures.

8. Approach activities with a certain selfishness. This is not to say that you must be concerned only with yourself, but you ought not to be so concerned with your position in the eyes of others that you are unable to accomplish anything new or original or fully engage in a particular activity. Look at your activities in relationship to what others think. Where the opinions of others are important to you, you have hit upon those crucial areas that can be most influenced by change in your mastery over yourself.

9. You can reduce negative feedback if you demonstrate courage, self-possession, and persistence without being swayed by circumstances.

10. Learn to recognize the effects of fears and that fear can be overcome by the information you have about its source—the responses and attitudes of others, for example. Fear generally arises from insufficient awareness of the goals of others. Knowledge of a situation will lead to mastery over it.

11. Learn that the most effective way to deal with fear or anxiety is through the acquisition of information and focused activity. If you implement what you have learned, you will demonstrate to yourself and to others that you are not overwhelmed by fear.

12. To some extent, knowledge means study of a particular task plus the actual effort of testing it. Failure in this sense yields information; you can return to the task with greater expertise the next time. The same principle obtains for criticism that, however unpleasant, can provide valuable information about ways to improve.

13. Don't dwell on potential sources of difficulty beyond the limited amount of information available to you. Lack of information will only magnify your illusions of fear and anxiety.

14. How you handle an anxiety-producing situation—either on the job, in the home, or in the community—will depend on your own particular temperament, constitution, and general way of handling things. You should not resort to a mechanical formula that is applicable to others, but must search for the particular method most compatible with your own particular way of life. This is a difficult lesson to learn. Most people emulate others in their conduct of life rather than mastering ways suited to themselves. New situations require new solutions. In your interaction with

new situations, the best approach for you will emerge. Remember that the more you look for solutions on your own, and the more you render the final judgment on the basis of your own assessment of a situation, the stronger you will be.

15. If you conceive of yourself as acting on behalf of your goals, you will muster strength and the capacity for dealing with the most complex situations. Acting with your goals in mind will minimize the psychological threats of specific situations.

16. Others may approach you for favors or advice, believing you are obligated to help. Be sure that when you do help others, it is out of genuine desire to do so rather than out of a sense of obligation, which will ultimately make you resentful and tense, consciously or unconsciously.

17. Continually master your daily activities. Act of your own accord, recognizing that ultimately the only things you can accomplish pertain not to the attitudes of others, but to your ability to be true to yourself. In this way, your life will be more rewarding and your conflicts will be minimized. Stick to what you find most rewarding.

18. Focus on the positive, and eliminate negative thoughts. You can think of only one thing at a time. If you focus on negative thoughts, you will develop a negative attitude and will be inhibited from action, which will further reinforce your negativism.

19. Relationships are strongest when they develop in pursuit of a shared objective or activity. Relationships that focus on simply "having a relationship" will prove taxing, frustrating, and generally unrewarding.

20. Where differences exist in attitude, values, and objectives, do not try to modify the other person to suit your needs. Similarly, don't allow yourself to be so accommodating that you compromise your own identity.

Find shared interests and activities and pursue these.

21. Above all, don't blame your own inaction on the other person and take credit for sacrificing your goals on his behalf. This is demeaning to him, and may in fact make him insecure about your true feelings. Do not compromise your interests to minimize his anger with you. Remember, when others are angry or feel you are letting them down when you pursue your interests, they are still better off than when they subconsciously fantasize about your unwillingness.

22. Don't feel obligated to continually reveal yourself to others. They will know your thoughts and attitudes from your actions. Make an effort to find time for solitude, when you can gather your strength and focus on your direction.

Appendix 2

Instructions for Patients on Medicine

1. You are being treated to help you overcome depression. Do not hesitate to accept such treatment and do not become discouraged if results seem slow in coming. Above all, do not blame yourself for what is happening, but regard this as you would any other ailment.
2. Follow the treatment to the letter. Inadequate attention to the physician's recommendations may not only delay recovery but prevent it.
3. Specifically, do not stop taking, decrease, or increase your medication unless directed to do so by the physician.
4. Keep a record of all medication taken. Should it be necessary to take other medicine from another physician, surgeon, dentist, or optometrist, such a record should be shown to him. It will ensure that undesirable mixtures of drugs will not be prescribed and that the appearance of drug-induced side effects will be understood.

5. Avoid all forms of alcohol. Alcohol may produce undesirable side effects or complications that may diminish the effectiveness of your medication. Certain foods, too, must be avoided when taking some types of antidepressant medication. It is important to follow the recommendations of the physician in these matters.

6. New and unusual symptoms of any kind must be reported to the physician, no matter how unrelated they may seem to your condition or how easily explained. Such a symptom may be a side effect of the drug you are taking. It is important that the physician be made aware of this, so that he can adjust your medication accordingly.

7. Also report any significant change of mood, appetite, sleep pattern, energy, ability to concentrate, or other function so that its severity can be assessed and appropriate treatment considered.

8. Avoid making any major life changes until discussing them with the physician, who may be better able to assess the decision objectively.

9. Do not take on unnecessary burdens while undergoing treatment until it is apparent to the physician that you are ready to do so.

Appendix 3

Life Crisis Inventory

GENERAL INSTRUCTIONS

This inventory has been developed* to yield data relevant to the clinical management of the patient and to test a range of important research questions. Originally focused on recent suicide attempts, it has been found useful with patients suffering from a variety of psychological disorders, including drug and alcohol abuse.

Data are collected through the use of a semistructured nondirective interview. The inventory is constructed to conform to the general flow of a clinical interview in a crisis situation. It has been designed to combine, as much as possible, the best elements of an open-ended clinical interview and a straightforward questionnaire. It relies heavily on the interviewer's skill to make clinical judgments on the basis of gathering a diversity of facts, attitudes, and impressions in various settings and under a variety of circumstances. The amount of information obtained will of course vary

---

*Developed with the assistance of Jane R. Slavin, C.S.W.

with the circumstances, the location of the interview, and the person being interviewed. The ratings must sometimes be made on the basis of inferences. However, they must always be recorded.* The reliability of the ratings will be assessed periodically by standard procedures. To facilitate data processing the inventory has been designed to directly code sixty major items which have been found to be most important. Demographic items have not been precoded as investigators using this inventory in other centers may have their preferences of data they wish to collect and subgroups they will focus on.

The Narrative (recorded on a separate sheet) is the detailed recording of the patient's view of his difficulties and why he is seeking help. It should include all information about the primary problem, such as a recent suicide attempt, depressive illness, drug abuse, alcoholism and/or interpersonal difficulties with which the patient is unable to cope. With the exception of the symptom section and specific information sought in the body of the questionnaire, all ratings are made on the basis of the information elicited and recorded at this time. Where information is obtained from other sources, such as an emergency room report, please note this on the form.

Suggested interview probes:

> Will you tell me what brought you here? What happened?
>
> When did you first feel something was wrong?
>
> Was there a progressive build-up of problems or symptoms?
>
> Could you tell me about the circumstances or sequence of events that led to your feeling depressed (or attempting suicide, taking drugs, drinking)?
>
> Do you feel you needed professional help?
>
> Do you think you are ill?

---

*If not applicable, score 0

Patient's Name: _____

Clinic Number: _____

SYMPTOMS*:

Explore the psychiatric symptoms experienced by patients during the current week. Ratings are made on the basis of instructions given for each item. Where applicable, make a notation.

1	2	3	4	5	6
NONE	MINIMAL	MILD	MODERATE	SEVERE	EXTREME

SOMATIC CONCERN	Degree of concern over present bodily health. Rate the degree to which physical health is perceived as a problem by the patient. Do not rate on basis of whether complaints have a realistic basis or not.	01
ANXIETY	Worry, fear, or overconcern for present or future. Rate solely on the basis of verbal report of patient's own subjective experiences. Do not infer anxiety from physical signs or from neurotic defense mechanisms.	02
EMOTIONAL WITHDRAWAL	Deficiency in relating to the interview situation. Rate only the degree to which the patient gives the impression of failing to be in emotional contact with other people in the interview situation.	03
CONCEPTUAL DISORGANI-ZATION	Degree to which the thought processes are confused, disconnected, or disorganized. Rate on the basis of integration of the verbal products of the patient; do not rate on the basis of patient's subjective impression of his own level of functioning.	04

*Items 1 to 18
Brief Psychiatric Rating Scale
Department of Health Education and Welfare, Public Health Service,
National Institute of Mental Health

GUILT FEELINGS	Overconcern or remorse for past behavior. Rate on the basis of the patient's subjective experiences of guilt as evidenced by verbal report with appropriate affect; do not infer guilt feelings from depression, anxiety, or neurotic defenses.	05
TENSION	Physical and motor manifestations of tension, "nervousness," and heightened activation level. Tension should be rated solely on the basis of physical signs and motor behavior and not on the basis of subjective experiences of tension reported by the patient.	06
MANNERISMS AND POSTURING	Unusual and unnatural motor behavior, the type of motor behavior that causes certain mental patients to stand out in a crowd of normal people. Rate only abnormality of movements; do not rate simple heightened motor activity here.	07
GRANDIOSITY	Exaggerated self-opinion, conviction of unusual ability or powers. Rate only on the basis of patient's statements about himself or self-in-relation-to-others, not on the basis of his demeanor in the interview situation.	08
DEPRESSIVE MOOD	Despondency in mood, sadness. Rate only degree of despondency; do not rate on the basis of inferences concerning depression based upon general retardation and somatic complaints.	09
HOSTILITY	Animosity, contempt, belligerence, disdain for other people outside the interview situation. Rate solely on the basis of the verbal report of feelings and actions of the patient toward others; do not infer hostility from neurotic defenses, anxiety, nor somatic complaints. (Rate attitude toward interviewer under "uncooperativeness.")	10
SUSPICIOUSNESS	Belief (delusional or otherwise) that others have now, or have had in the past, malicious or discriminatory intent toward the patient. On the basis of verbal report,	

	rate only those suspicions that are cur- rently held whether they concern past or_____ present circumstances.	11
HALLUCIN- ATORY BEHAVIOR	Perceptions without normal external stim- ulus correspondence. Rate only those ex- periences that are reported to have oc- curred within the last week and that are described as distinctly different from the thought and imagery processes of normal_____ people.	12
MOTOR RETARDATION	Reduction in energy level evidenced in slowed movements. Rate on the basis of observed behavior of the patient only; do not rate on basis of patient's subjective_____ impression of own energy level.	13
UNCO- OPERATIVE- NESS	Evidence of resistance, unfriendliness, re- sentment, and lack of readiness to cooper- ate with the interviewer. Rate only on the basis of the patient's attitude and re- sponses to the interviewer and the inter- view situation; do not rate on basis of re- ported resentment or uncooperativeness_____ outside the interview situation.	14
UNUSUAL THOUGHT CONTENT	Unusual, odd, strange, or bizarre thought content. Rate here the degree of unusual- ness, not the degree of disorganization of_____ thought processes.	15
BLUNTED AFFECT	Reduced emotional tone, apparent lack of_____ normal feeling or involvement.	16
EXCITEMENT	Heightened emotional tone, agitation, in-_____ creased reactivity.	17
DISORIEN- TATION	Confusion or lack of proper association_____ for person, place, or time.	18
SLEEP	Inability to fall asleep, early morning awakening, interrupted sleep pattern. Rate only if this is different from pa- tient's usual pattern. Do not make rating_____ for excessive sleep.	19
APPETITE AND/OR WEIGHT LOSS	Loss of interest in food, can be accom- panied by loss of weight. Rate only on the basis of what patient reports is a change_____ in his usual pattern.	20

SEXUAL FUNCTIONING	Loss of interest, enjoyment and inability to perform-respond. Rate on the basis of a change in pattern as reported by the patient.	21
SUICIDAL THOUGHTS	Includes thoughts about death, wanting to die or to end all suffering. Rating is made on the extent to which these thoughts preoccupy the patient during waking hours.	22
COMPULSIVE BEHAVIOR	Uncontrollable need to repeat the same action, e.g., touching, counting, washing hands. Rate only on the basis of a verbal report of the presence and degree behavior interferes with patient's functioning.	23
OBSESSIONAL THOUGHTS	An idea that persists in the mind of the individual that cannot be gotten rid of by a conscious process. The thought is uninfluenced by logic or reasoning and is distinctly unwanted. Rate on the basis of patient's report of his subjective experience.	24

		Yes	No
OTHER SYMPTOMS	_____	1	2
	_____		
	_____		25

SICK ROLE: The patient's view of his symptoms and difficulties and willingness to accept treatment.

On the basis of what the patient reports, use the following scale to rate the patient in terms of accepting the sick role.

1   Medical model
     He is suffering from an illness that has a biophysiological chemical base. Symptoms and cause are not controllable through his own efforts, he gave up most responsibilities, he accepts treatment, and believes the doctor will help him.

2   Psychiatric model
    Psychological illness caused by unknown mental factors, he doesn't blame self, but feels he has some part to play. Relieved of some responsibility, i.e., took vacation because of how he was feeling. Needs treatment.
3   Psychological model
    Recognizes emotional illness results from neurosis. Lessens activities, reluctantly accepts treatment.
4   Psychoanalytic model
    Not illness but reaction to parents and traumatic experiences. Sees self as mainly responsible for cure; refuses medication. Is concerned with major personality change, growth, and maturation.
5   Situational model
    No illness; current events caused difficulties. Blames self for inability to cope, and wants to exert more will-power. No belief in psychiatric treatment for self, only others.
6   Denial model
    No illness; nothing wrong. Continues all activities, refuses treatment, has no belief in psychiatric help.   26

THE ATTEMPT

This section explores the patient's suicidal behavior at the time of the attempt.

1	2	3	4	5	6
NONE	MINIMAL	MILD	MODERATE	SEVERE	EXTREME

If Not Applicable, Score Items 27-35   0

DEGREE OF DISCOMFORT—Was the patient aware of experiencing discomfort such as depressed mood, delusional ideas, heightened excitability or feeling empty? The degree and duration of discomfort is included in the judgment.

On the basis of what the patient indicates, rate as follows:

A one rating—patient felt calm and unaware of any emotional or physical distress before the attempt.

A three rating—patient was feeling down, somewhat uncomfortable on day of the attempt.

A five rating—patient felt overwhelmed for more than two days, convinced there was no hope of feeling better.   27

IMPULSIVITY—How long did the patient think about what he would do? Did he have clear thoughts of death or of hurting himself or was the act simply done to relieve extreme tension? The important determinant is the length of time between thought, decision, and behavior. This rating considers preparation, premeditation of self-destruction, plans for after the act such as a will.

A one rating—patient had elaborate plans, put everything in order, chose time, place, and date for death.

A three rating—patient wrote a note, thought for an hour, then took pills.

A five rating—patient woke up, was very tense, went to get razor blades, moments passed before act. No real conceptualized death wishes.   28

SUICIDAL ACT

Patient's choice of method, attitude, intention to die, as well as the outcome of the attempt.

Judgment is based on prior exploration of degree of discomfort, impulsivity, as well as specific information explored around intent and dangerousness of act. Rating explanations can be used as probes where needed.

METHOD

1	2	3	4	5	6	
Pills	Lacerations	Gas	Poison	Jump	Gun	
						29

PLACE

1	2	3	4	5	6	
Home	Friend's House	Work	Park	Bridge	Rented Rm.	
						30

PROXIMITY OF OTHER PEOPLE

1	2	3	
Close	Easily Accessible	Distant	
			31

PHYSICAL RESULTS

None	Present	Undetermined
0	1	2

_____

_____

_____

                                                                                 32

Type of substance ingested _____
Amount _____

PATIENT TRIED TO REVERSE SITUATION?

Not Determined	Yes	No	
0	1	2	
			33

PATIENT'S ACTIONS:

1	2	3
Told someone immediately	Went to hospital	Called hospital or doctor

4	5	6
Called suicide-prevention service	Waited for someone who might come	Did nothing

_____
34

RATING OF SUICIDAL ACT (Intent and Danger)

1 No suicidal intent or physical effect.
2 Accidental poisoning or overdose in confused state as from drunkenness or from habit of taking pills. Little or no effect of drug ingested—superficial cut wrist.
3 Intent to injure self. Amount understood by patient to be nondeadly although physical effect could be sleep or drowsiness. Emergency medical care restricted to routine admission procedures, stitches required.
4 Intent to injure self. Amount of drug adequate to produce coma, without change in vital signs or mechanical support. Patient took active steps to ensure convenient help that will certainly come.
5 Strong intent to injure self and amount of drug large/as much as patient has available. Patient's physical response comatose or equivalent. Some support of vital functions not exceeding 30 minutes. Chance determines if help will come.
6 Strongest intent to kill self. Type and amount of drug understood to be deadly. Method high lethality, e.g. shotgun. Physical condition requires mechanical and physiological support of more than 30 minutes. Blood transfusion. Major surgical procedure required.

_____
35

PREVIOUS ATTEMPTS

Note number, when, and under what circumstances. Give a rating of one point for each attempt.

_____

_____   36

_____

DRUG USAGE

Substances Used   Amount Frequency Duration
Marijuana _____
Hash _____
Opium _____
LSD _____
DMT _____
THC _____
Peyote _____
Mescaline _____
Heroin _____
Cocaine _____
Other _____

INTERVIEWERS RATING OF DRUG BEHAVIOR

1   None
2   Occasional use of marijuana in social settings
    such as party.
3   Periodic entry into the drug subculture. Use
    of a variety of substances, such as stimulants
    and hallucinogens.
4   Frequent use of a variety of drugs including
    amphetamines, hallucinogens, opiates, and
    barbiturates. Drug usage has become a
    major focal point in his life.
5   Habitual use of amphetamines, hallucino-
    gens, and/or heroin. Drug usage has begun

to interfere with major relationships and activities.

6   Psychologically and physiologically addicted   ___
    to heroin or other opiate derivative.   37

ALCOHOL USAGE

1   None, never drinks.
2   Occasional drink at social functions.
3   Social drinker, after work, at parties and dinners.
4   Uses alcohol regularly to calm self or to continue functioning or active A.A. member.
5   Alcohol intake is sufficient to interfere with job performance, cause absences. Job instability directly related to drinking habits.
6   Addicted to alcohol. Has been or should consider A.A. Life is focused around drinking.   ___
                                                       38

LETHALITY

Based on the following scales the patient is rated in terms of his suicidalness (i.e. the possibility of his making a suicide attempt in the near future).

39. SUICIDAL THOUGHTS	40. THREATS	41. PREPARATORY BEHAVIOR	
1 None	1 None	1 None	
2 Occasional thoughts—passive	2 Expression of suicidal thoughts	2 Reading up on various methods	
3 Recurrent thoughts	3 Verbal threats in the presence of others	3 Inquiries about lethality of pills	
4 Active, persistent, obsessional thoughts, ego syntonic	4 Russian, roulette, threats about future behavior	4 Stockpiling	___ 39
5 Persistent, not ego dystonic thoughts, plans	5 Beginning to act out suicidal intention	5 Last will closing affairs	___ 40

6	Delusional, voices telling patient to kill self; conviction of guilt; need to punish by death	6	In the process of suicidal act in the presence of others	6	Lethal method arranged

41

OVERALL RATING OF LETHALITY
1 None
2 Minimum. The presence of occasional thoughts, no other behavior.
3 Gesture in response to interpersonal conflict. There might have been threats in the heat of anger or peak of disappointment. No prior plans.
4 Threats in form of behavior. Thoughts may also have been present. Patient is considered a character-disorder; past history includes self destructive behavior and/or violent acts toward others.
5 Patient has well thought out plans, told others about a desire to die, is socially isolated; elderly depressed male.
6 Delusional ideation about necessity of death, patient has enough pills or other means to kill self. Is chronically depressed or schizophrenic and has a history of a recent major attempt.

42

PSYCHOSOCIAL HISTORY AND CURRENT LIFESTYLE

These ratings are based on a discussion with the patient about his relationships with relatives, friends, coworkers, neighbors, as well as his contact with major social institutions such as churches, clubs, associations and department of social welfare. The significant material can be recorded in the spaces provided. Ratings are based on the interviewer's subjective assessment of the patient. It is important that the important factual data be recorded.

SIGNIFICANT OTHER RELATIONSHIP

1 Close. Not a contributing factor.
2 Close. Some minor dissatisfactions. Did not contribute to the patient's difficulties, but did not support the patient.
3 Somewhat distant.
4 Threatened change of status or characterized by overdependence.
5 Offers little positive rewards in terms of mental health. Strong sadomasochistic factors present.
6 Relationship is pathological and has definite relationship to patient's symptom formation.

—
43

INTERPERSONAL CONFLICT

1 None.
2 Some conflict with others.
3 Conflicts in most relationships but do not prevent the patient from making friends or maintaining present relationships.
4 Frequent conflict with those close to patient. Some conflict with friends and coworkers.
5 Severe and long-standing conflicts characterize close relationships.
6 Conflicts pose a definite threat to patient's emotional well-being and physical safety.

—
44

DEGREE OF ISOLATION

Patient lives alone.	1	2
	Yes	No

1 None.
2 Has close family ties. Little contact with friends.

3 Frequently in contact with others on the job, social activities. No close relationships.
4 Minimal contact with others. Schizoid pattern of functioning, spends most of his or her time alone with intellectual or manual pursuits.
5 Contacts with others in formal settings such as work or social agency, or patient has lost all significant relatives and friends as in the case of old people living alone.
6 Almost no outside contacts, except in form of news dealer, storekeeper, etc. Person would be considered a recluse.

45

OBJECTIVE STRESSES WITHIN LAST 12 MONTHS

1 None.
2 Minimal stressful event.
3 Mild stress, e.g. organizational shifts or planned residential relocation.
4 Moderate stress such as threatened separation from spouse, financial loss curtailing family or individual activities or purchasing power.
5 Severe stress from point of view of the significance of the event or modification in lifestyle to patient, e.g. forced retirement.
6 Severe objective stress, e.g., loss of limb, death of significant other, terminal illness of patient or significant others.

46

Specify nature and intensity of stress, its duration and the patient's reaction.

_____

_____

_____

_____

NOTEWORTHY BEHAVIOR PATTERNS

1   None.
2   Occasional drinking, promiscuity, taking drugs such as marijuana.
3   Has taken barbiturates, LSD, speed as part of socializing; some excessive drinking or promiscuity.
4   Occasional sexual deviation, e.g. homosexuality. Regular use of heavy drugs, alcoholic intake has caused occasional blackouts, interfered with work. Has been arrested for misdemeanors.
5   Overall adjustment deviant, drugs, alcohol, sexual, criminal record.
6   Addicted to alcohol/drugs. Served long prison term. Has severe sexual problem from viewpoint of society—perversions resulted in criminal charges or arrests.   47

Specify nature, frequency, and consequence of such behavior.

_____
_____
_____
_____

FAMILY BACKGROUND

        Sibling Rank
        Only Child   Yes   No
        Parents Separated   Yes   No   Patient's Age _____
        Parents Divorced   Yes   No   Patient's Age _____

1   Stable family life.
2   Some conflict in the home.
3   Family instability such as periodic separations, frequent residential moves, alcoholism.

4　Definite deprivation, poverty, divorce, abandonment.
5　Severe psychiatric illness, suicide attempts in the immediate family; traumatic childhood.
6　History of chronic mental illness in parental family: close relative, mother, father, sibling completed suicide.　— 48

OVERALL FUNCTIONING

Specify employment status, nature of work, performance, special stresses.

1　Within normal limits.
2　Symptoms have had some effect on functioning, e.g. takes longer to complete tasks.
3　Patient has been having difficulty meeting all responsibilities, e.g. has stopped socializing because of fatigue or lack of time.
4　Difficulties have extended to a major responsibility such as work, e.g. sick-leave increased, housework not done.
5　Symptoms have resulted in lack of performance. Patient spends a great deal of time in bed or sitting, has no interest in self or activities. Has been fired.
6　Pervasiveness of symptoms requires hospitalization.　— 49

DIAGNOSTIC IMPRESSIONS

(Describe the patient in narrative form)

_____

_____

_____

_____

_____

_____

	1	2	3	
Diagnosis	Psychosis	Character Disorder	Depression	50

PROGNOSIS

On the basis of what is known about the patient, the interviewer subjectively predicts what the patient's condition will be after one year.

1 Much better; no significant remaining psychological problems.
2 Better; improved to premorbid functions.
   a. mental status
   b. life situation
3 Some improvement; no attempt.
4 Same. Still suicidal risk on basis of persistent thoughts, gestures, attempts.
5 Worse. Increased severity of symptoms, increase in impaired functioning, repeat attempts, life situation worse in observer's judgment.
6 Dead from attempt.
7 Dead from natural causes.   51

RELIABILITY OF PATIENT

1	2	3
good	questionable	unreliable

SIGNIFICANT OTHER FORM

Name: _____ Telephone _____
Address: _____

_____

Relationship to Patient:

0	1	2	3
Not Applicable	spouse	parent	sibling

4	5	6	
roommate	friend	other	52

Attitude Toward Patient—Reaction to Patient

	1	2	3	4	
Current:	supportive	fearful	resentful	rejecting	53
	1	2	3	4	
In the Past:	supportive	indifferent	hostile	rejecting	54

DESCRIPTION OF OVERALL RELATIONSHIP

1 Close; not a contributing factor in precipitating crisis.
2 Close; some minor dissatisfaction, not a contributing factor to the patient's difficulties but did not support the patient.
3 Somewhat distant; this may have played a part in exacerbating patient's difficulties.
4 Threatened change of status coincided with crisis situation; relationship characterized by overdependence.
5 Offers little positive rewards in terms of mental health; strong sadomasochistic factors present.
6 Relationship is pathological and directly related to patient's symptom formation.   55

DEGREE OF CONFLICT

1 None.
2 Some.
3 Conflict does not threaten relationship although it is frequent.
4 Conflict is frequent and threatens the continuation of relationship.
5 Severe; long-standing problem; great concern; separations may have occurred.

6   Conflicts pose a definite threat to the pa-   —
    tient's physical and emotional well-being.   56

SIGNIFICANT OTHER'S EVALUATION OF PATIENT

ISOLATION

1   None.
2   Has close family ties; little contact with
    others on the job or through social activities.
3   Frequently in contact with others; no close
    relationships.
4   Minimal contact with others; schizoid pattern
    of functioning; spends most of the time alone
    in intellectual or manual pursuits.
5   Has contact with others as at work or with a
    social agency; lost all significant relatives; in-
    formant's relationship is on a "good samari-
    tan" basis.
6   Almost no outside contacts except in form of
    newspaper dealer, storekeeper, etc.; is con-   —
    sidered a recluse.   57

OVERALL FUNCTIONING

1   Good.
2   Symptoms have had an effect on functioning;
    e.g. it takes longer to complete a task.
3   Patient has been having difficulty meeting
    most of his responsibilities, e.g. has stopped
    socializing because of fatigue or lack of time.
4   Difficulties have extended to major responsi-
    bility such as work, e.g. sick-leave increased,
    housework not done.
5   Symptoms have resulted in total lack of per-

formance; patient has spent most of his time
in bed.

6   Aware of pervasiveness of symptoms; thinks
    patient needs to be in a hospital.

__
58

RESPONSE TO THE ATTEMPT (OR CRISIS SITUATION)

Notes—Record details of significant other's ac-
       tivities, emotional reaction, and efforts to
       obtain help.

1   Was with patient; knew what to do in the
    way of first aid, or sought immediate pro-
    fessional assistance where needed.

2   Was contacted by the patient; arranged for
    immediate help; went to where patient was,
    without much delay.

3   Was able to direct patient how to seek help
    for self; did not think it necessary to go to
    patient; made a follow-up call to see how pa-
    tient was.

4   Became anxious; unable to do anything until
    some time passed; however did not place pa-
    tient in danger of serious physical damage.

5   Was confused, overwhelmed; delay in getting
    assistance could have prevented patient's re-
    covery; someone else intervened.

6   Was in a panic state; needed assistance for
    self; chance determined that help was given
    to the patient.

__
59

Notes:

_____
_____
_____
_____

SICK ROLE

On the basis of what significant other reports, use the following scale to rate their view of the patient's problem in terms of accepting the sick role.

1   Medical model
    He is suffering from an illness that has a bio-physiological chemical base. Symptoms and cause are not controllable through own efforts. Gave up most responsibilities. Accepts treatment, believes doctor will help him.

2   Psychiatric model
    Psychological illness caused by unknown mental factors, doesn't blame self but feels he has some part to play. Relieved of some responsibility, i.e., took vacation because of how he was feeling. Needs treatment.

3   Psychological model
    Recognizes emotional illness results from neurosis. Lessens activities, reluctantly accepts treatment.

4   Psychoanalytic model
    Not illness but reaction to parents and traumatic experiences. Expects long-term treatment with no guarantee, sees self as mainly responsible for cure, refuses medication.

5   Situational model
    No illness, current events caused difficulties. Blames self for inability to cope and wants to exert more will-power. No belief in psychiatric treatment for self, only others.

6   Denial model
    No illness, nothing wrong, continues all activities, refuses treatment, has no belief in psychiatric help.

___

60

References

Adler, Alfred. *Problems of Neurosis.* New York: Harper and Row, 1964.

Arieff, A., McCullough, R., and Rotman, D. B. "Unsuccessful Suicidal Attempts." *Diseases of the Nervous System* 9:179, 1948.

Baldwin, A. L., Kalhorn, J., and Breese, F. H. "Patterns of Parent Behavior." *Psychologic Monographs* 58:No. 3, 1948.

Batchelor, I. R. C., and Napier, M. B. "The Sequelae and Short-Term Prognosis of Attempted Suicide." *Journal of Neurology, Neuro-Surgery and Psychiatry* 17:263, 1964.

Cavan, R. S., Burgess, E. W., Havighurst, R. J., and Goldhamer, H. *Personal Adjustment in Old Age.* Chicago: Science Research Ass., 1949.

Chafetz, Morris E. *Liquor: The Servant of Man.* Boston: Little, Brown, 1965.

147

Delong, B., and Robbins, E. "The Communication of Suicidal Intent Prior to Psychiatric Hospitalization." *American Journal of Psychiatry* 117:695, 1961.

Dorpat, T. A., and Boswell, J. W. "Evaluation of Suicidal Intent in Suicidal Attempts." *Comprehensive Psychiatry* 4:120, 1963.

Dorpat, T. A., and Ripley, H. S. "Study of Suicide in Kings County, Washington." *Northwest Medicine* 61, 1962.

Dublin, L. J. *Suicide: A Sociological and Statistical Study.* New York: Ronald Press, 1963.

Durkheim, E. *Suicide.* New York: Free Press, 1951.

Eisenthal, X., Farberow, N. L., and Schneidman, E. "Follow-up of Neuropsychiatric Patients in Suicide Observation Status." *Public Health Report* 81:977, 1966.

Ettlinger, R., and Flordh, P. "Attempted Suicide." *Acta Psychiatrica Scandinavia* 103:5, 1955.

Farberow, N. L., and McEvoy, T. L. "Suicide Among Patients with Diagnoses of Anxiety Reaction or Depressive Reaction in General, Medical and Surgical Hospitals." *Journal of Abnormal Psychology* 71:287, 1966.

Farberow, N. L., and Schneidman, E. "Attempted, Threatened and Completed Suicide." *Journal of Abnormal and Social Psychology* 50:230, 1955.

Farberow, N. L., and Schneidman, E. *Cry for Help.* New York: McGraw-Hill, 1961.

Fisch, M. "The Suicide Gesture: A Study of 144 Military Patients Hospitalized Because of Abortive Suicide Attempts." *American Journal of Psychiatry* 111:35, 1954.

Freud, Sigmund. *Standard Edition of the Complete Psychological Works.* London: Hogarth Press, 1953–1965.

Gardner, E. A., Bahn, A. K., and Mack, M. "Suicide and Psychiatric Care in the Aging." *Archives of General Psychiatry* 10:522, 1964.

Gibbs, J. P. "Suicide." In R. K. Merton and R. A. Nisbet (eds.), *Contemporary Social Problems.* New York: Harcourt Brace and Company, 1961.

Gruenberg, E. M. Community Case-Finding Methods: Final Report to the Health Research Council of the City of New York, April 1, 1964–June 30, 1967.

Harman, H. H. *Modern Factor Analysis.* Chicago: University of Chicago Press, 1968, Table B, 435.

Hendin, Herbert. *Suicide and Scandinavia.* New York: Grune and Stratton, 1964.

Horney, Karen, *Our Inner Conflicts.* New York: Norton, 1945.

Hughes, C. C., Tremblay, M. A., Rapoport, R. N., and Leighton, A. *People of Cove and Woodlot.* 1960.

Idestiom and Von Reis. *Sv Lakartidn.* 48:2925, 1951.

Jansson, B. "A Catamnestic Study of 476 Attempted Suicides." *Acta Psychiatrica Scandinavica* 38:2925, 1962.

Jelliwek, E. M. *The Disease Concept of Alcoholism.* New Haven: Hillhouse Press, 1960.

Kessel, N., and Lee, E. M. "Attempted Suicide in Edinburgh." *Scottish Medical Journal* 7:130, 1962.

Kiev, A. (Ed.). *Magic, Faith and Healing.* New York: Free Press, 1964.

Kiev, A. *A Strategy for Daily Living.* New York: Free Press, 1964.

Kiev, A. *Curanderismo.* New York: Free Press, 1968.

Kiev, A. "Prognostic Factors in Attempted Suicide." *American Journal of Psychiatry* 131:987, 1974.

Kiev, A. "Psychotherapeutic Strategies in the Management of Depressed and Suicidal Patients." *American Journal of Psychotherapy* 29:345, 1975.

Kiev, A. "Symptom Patterns and the Acceptance of the 'Sick Role' in Attempted Suicide." *Current Medical Research and Opinion* 2, Suppl. 34:34, 1975.

Kiev, A. "Cluster Analysis Profiles of Suicide Attempters." *American Journal of Psychiatry* 132:63, 1976.

Kiorbo, E. *Journal of Gerontology* 6:233, 1951.

Krupinski, J., Polke, P., and Stoller, A. "Psychiatric Disturbances Attempted and Completed Suicides in Victoria during 1963." *Medical Journal of Australia* 52: 773, 1965.

Langner, T. S., and Michael, S. T. *Life Stress and Mental Health*. New York: Free Press of Glencoe, 1963.

Lavenson, G. S., Plum, F., and Swanson, A. G. "Physiological Management Compared with Pharmacological and Electrical Stimulation in Barbiturate Poisoning." *Journal of Pharmacology and Experimental Therapeutics* 122:271, 1958.

Leighton, A. *My Name Is Legion*. New York: Basic Books, Inc., 1959.

Leighton, D., Harding, J. S., Macklin, D. B., Macmillan, A. M., and Leighton, A. *The Character of Danger: The Striking County Study of Disorder and Sociocultural Environment*. New York: Basic Books, Inc., 1963.

Levi, L. D., Fales, C., Stein, M., and Sharp, V. H. "Separation and Attempted Suicide." *Archives of General Psychiatry* 158, 1966.

Litman, R. E., and Farberow, N. L. "Emergency Evaluation of Self-Destructive Potentiality." In N. L. Farberow and E. Schneidman (eds.), *Cry for Help*. New York: McGraw-Hill, 1961.

Mechanic, David. *Medical Sociology*. New York: Free Press, 1968.

Menninger, Karl. *Man Against Himself*. New York: Harcourt Brace, 1938.

Moss, L., and Hamilton, D. "The Psychotherapy of Suicidal Patients." *American Journal of Psychiatry* 112: 814, 1956.

Motto, Jerome A. "Suicide Attempts: A Longitudinal View." *Archives of General Psychiatry* 13:516, 1965.

Oliven, J. P. "The Suicide Risk." *New England Journal of Medicine* 245:488, 1951.

O'Neal, P., Robbins, E., and Schmidt, E. H. "A Psychiatric Study of Attempted Suicides in Persons Over Sixty Years of Age." *Archives of Neurology and Psychiatry* 75:275, 1956.

Parsons, T. *The Social System.* Glencoe: The Free Press, 1951.

Plum, F. "Management of Acute Depressive Drug Poisoning." In *Cecil and Loeb Textbook of Medicine,* Edition 12:1505, 1967.

Plum, F., and Posner, N. B. *The Diagnosis of Stupor and Coma.* Philadelphia: F. A. Davis and Co., 1966.

Plum, F., and Swanson, A. G. "Barbiturate Poisoning Treated by Physiological Methods." *Journal of American Medical Association* 163:827, 1957.

Polals, A., and Plum, F. "Comparison of a New Analeptic in Barbiturate Poisoned Animals." *Journal of Pharmacology and Experimental Therapeutics* 145:27, 1964.

Raines, G., and Thomson, S. "Suicides: Some Basic Considerations." *Digest of Neurology and Psychiatry* 18:101, 1950.

Richardson, S. A., Dohrenwend, B., and Klein, D. *Interviewing: Its Forms and Functions.* New York: Basic Books, Inc., 1965.

Robbins, S., Gassner, J., Kayes, R., and Wilkinson, R. "The Communication of Suicidal Intent: A Study of 134 Consecutive Cases of Successful (Completed) Suicide." *American Journal of Psychiatry* 115:724, 1959.

Rubenstein, R., Moses, R., and Lidz, T. "On Attempted

Suicide." *Archives of Neurology and Psychiatry* 79: 103, 1958.

Rutter, M., and Brown, G. W. "The Measurement of Family Activities and Relationships in Families Containing a Psychiatric Patient." *Social Psychiatry* 1:38, 1966.

Rutter, M., and Brown, G. W. "The Reliability and Validity of Measures of Family Life and Relationships in Families Containing a Psychiatric Patient." *Social Psychiatry* 1:38, 1966.

Sainsbury, P. *Suicide in London.* New York: Basic Books, 1956.

Shagass, C., and Schwartz, M. "Excitability of the Cerebral Cortex in Psychiatric Disorders." In R. Roessler and N. S. Greenfield (eds.), *Physiological Correlates of Psychological Disorders.* Madison: University of Wisconsin Press, 1962, pp. 45–60.

Shneidman, E., and Farberow, N. L. "Statistical Comparisons Between Attempted and Committed Suicides." In E. Shneidman and N. L. Farberow (eds.), *Cry for Help.* New York: McGraw Hill, 1961.

Spitzer, R. L., Endicott, J., and Fleiss, J. L. "Instruments and Recording Forms for Evaluating Psychiatric Status and History: Rationale, Method of Development and Description." (Unpublished paper, 1967.)

Spitzer, R. L., Fleiss, J. L., Endicott, J., and Cohen, J. "Mental Status Schedule." *Archives of General Psychiatry* 16:479, 1967.

Srole, L., Langer, T. S., Michael, S. T., Opler, M. K., and Rennie, T. A. C. *Mental Health in the Metropolis: The Midtown Manhattan Study.* New York: McGraw-Hill, 1962.

Stengel, E. "Attempted Suicide." *Proceedings of the Royal Society of Medicine* 45:613, 1952.

Stengel, E. "Recent Research into Suicide and Attempted Suicide." *American Journal of Psychiatry* 118:725, 1962.

Stengel, E., and Cook, N. *Attempted Suicide.* Oxford: Oxford University Press, 1958.

Sullivan, H. S. *Interpersonal Theory of Psychiatry* (ed. by H.S. Perry and M. L. Gawel) New York: Norton, 1953.

Tabachnick, N. "Interpersonal Relationships in Suicide Attempts." *Archives of General Psychiatry* 4:16, 1961.

Tabachnick, N., and Farberow, N. L. "The Assessment of Self-Destructive Potentiality." In N. Farberow and E. Shneidman (eds.), *Cry for Help.* New York: McGraw Hill, 1961.

Toolan, James. "Suicide and Suicide Attempts." *American Journal of Psychiatry* 118:719, 1962.

Trautman, E. C. "Suicide Attempts of Puerto Rican Immigrants." *Psychiatric Quarterly* 35:3, 1961.

Vital Statistics by Health Areas and Health Center Districts. Bureau of Records and Statistics, New York City Department of Health, 1961, 1962, 1963, 1964, and 1965.

Wall, James H. "The Psychiatric Problem of Suicides." *American Journal of Psychiatry* 101:404, 1944.

Weiss, J. "The Gamble with Death in Attempted Suicide." *Psychiatry* 20:17, 1957.

Wilson, E. "Treatment of Barbiturate Intoxication." *Acta Medica Scandinavica* 139: Supplement 253, 1951.

Zubin, Joseph. "A Biometric Approach to the Classification of Suicidal Behavior." Delivered before "Workshop on Measurement of Suicidal Behavior," October 14, 15, 1971, Penn. Center Inn, Pennsylvania.

Index

About the author

Ari Kiev, M.D., is Clinical Associate Professor of Psychiatry at Cornell University Medical College and head of the Cornell Program in Social Psychiatry. He also is in private practice as a psychiatrist.

After completing his undergraduate work at Harvard, Dr. Kiev attended Cornell, where he earned his M.D. degree.

The author is a member of the American Medical Association, the American Psychiatric Association, the Royal Medico-Psychological Association, and the Association for Applied Anthropology. He is on the editorial boards of several professional journals, has published numerous articles, and is the author of four books.